Evolving Intentions
in
Public Art

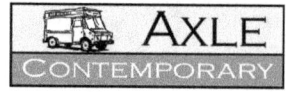

Published by
Axle Contemporary Press
P.O. Box 22095
Santa Fe NM 87502
www.axlepress.com

ISBN 978-0-9858116-9-3

Photo Credits:

Matthew Chase Daniel – 16, 21, 22, 26, 35, 193, 195
Nina Mastrangelo – 34, 205
Chrissie Orr – 38, 41, 46, 49
Christy Hengst – 128, 131, 132, 137, 138, 140
Jerry Wellman – 148, 150
Emily Schiffer – 153 (top)
Angele E. Essemba – 153 (middle)
Sophie Rousmaniere – 153 (bottom)
Oumarou Mebouack – 171
Kate Russell – 209
Caity Kennedy – 157, 165, 226
Helmut Hillenkamp – 12, 88 (top), 146, 169, 176, 186, 202, 215, 221, 229, back cover
Genevieve Russell 135, 145

This book is made possible by Axle Projects, Inc. which is funded by individual donations, and grants from the City of Santa Fe's 1% Lodgers' Tax, The Caprock Fund of the Tides Foundation, The McCune Charitable Foundation, and New Mexico Arts, a division of the Department of Cultural Affairs, and the National Endowment for the Arts.

Evolving Intentions
in
Public Art

a symposium
produced by

Christy Hengst
The Kathryn Street Arts Festival
The Center for Contemporary Arts
Axle Contemporary

Santa Fe, New Mexico
September 13, 2014

Table of Contents

See slideshows and videos from the symposium at:
www.evolvingintentionsinpublicart.org

PREFACE

I remember when in 1994, as a younger artist, I participated in a "public art apprenticeship" with Suzanne Lacy at Anderson Ranch in Colorado. It was part of a week-long extravaganza of workshops, performances, and panel discussions delving in to "the new public art", with a bunch of artists like Mel Chin, Judy Baca, Rachel Rosenthal... Wow, what adventure! New ways of thinking, new questions, crossing disciplines, creating new roadmaps in art -- it was exhilarating and overwhelming.

It took a while for me personally to digest, try out some things, and eventually find my own way to create work that made sense coming from me, but I've always felt so grateful for the various glimpses into the experiences and processes of other people.

This little conference, "Evolving Intentions in Public Art," emerged partly out of that sentiment: The feeling that all of us, and especially people just coming up in the field, might be hungry to hear about the possibilities of creating your own map. Another motivation is more selfish than that, a vague feeling of isolation. Like many people, I've been raising kids and hanging in there with continued art practice, but haven't had much time to look left or right. I don't know so much about what other people have been doing, or even how what I've been doing might fit in to the larger context. I started dreaming of -- craving -- more actual conversation, specifically and deeply about questions of public art. In experimentation, and manifestation, what worked? What didn't? What was your goal? Is that still what you want? What meaning did you come out of it with? How meaningful do you think your project was for other people? What were the new questions that came up? It turns out, you just have to ask! Everybody I approached was interested in this conversation.

Santa Fe, in my opinion, has been living a kind of renaissance in the past decade of creative, out-of-the-box projects. Projects like Haiku Roadsign, El Otro Lado, Meow Wolf, Urban Way, Orphan Letters, Neighborhood Haikus, Snow Poems, Birds in the Park, Rivers Run Through Us, Lifesongs, and many more, finding their own format and way to reach the world. So we started with people based here in Santa Fe. Axle Contemporary stepped right up to co-sponsor the event, the Center for Contemporary Art offered their space to hold it in, and New Mexico Arts kindly gave a grant to create this archival book as a record of the discussion. It was very satisfying, I think to all involved. Personally, my respect for these artists and their intentions just grows and grows.
Meanwhile the event itself felt like the first installment, with more to come... we'll see.

The conference took place on Saturday, September 13th, at CCA in Santa Fe. The transcripts are pretty much exactly what was said (I cleaned up the "um"s and "so"s to make it more readable). Links to the videos and other visual material are at www.evolvingintentionsinpublicart.org. I hope you enjoy it!

Christy Hengst
February 2015
Santa Fe, NM

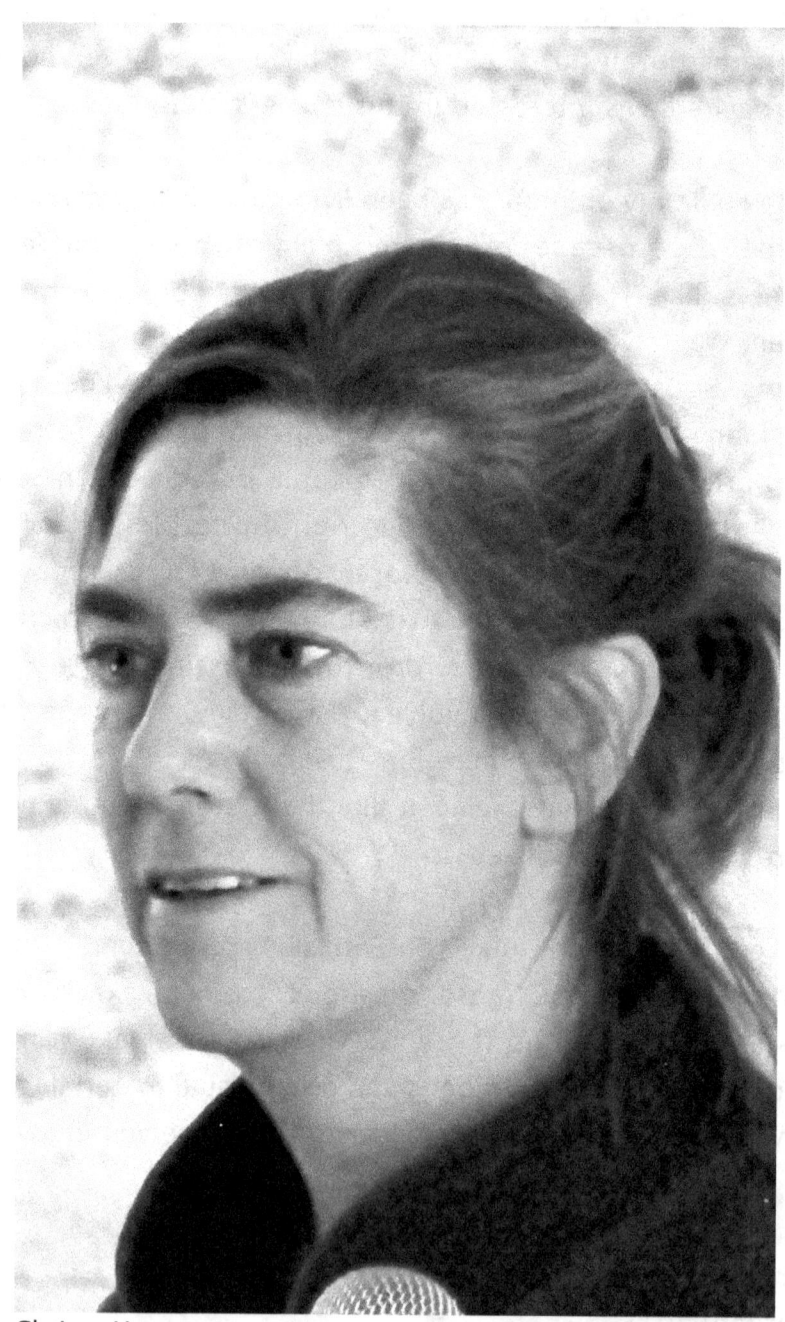

Christy Hengst

Christy Hengst:

Hi everybody, thank you so much for being here. This is a conversation that has been brewing for a long time, and I'm so excited that it's finally happening -- hopefully it's the first part of something ongoing.

This morning we're going to start with presentation of projects, and we'll be hearing from Matthew Chase-Daniel first about Gourdsigns, then Aly Kreikemeier will talk about El Otro Lado, then Molly Sturges is going to tell about about Lifesongs and COAL. We'll have a break and then Edie Tsong will talk about Snow Poems, Dominique Mazeaud and Bobbe Besold will present Rivers Run Through Us, and I'll talk about Birds in the Park.

Then we'll have a break for lunch, and in the afternoon it will be a rectangletable discussion with Alysha Shaw, Vince Kadlubek of Meow Wolf, Jerry Wellman of Axle Contemporary, Sanjit Sethi of the Santa Fe Art Institute, Issa Nyaphaga and Paula Castillo, moderated by Michelle Laflamme-Childs who used to work for the Art Institute and now is at New Mexico Arts.

Then in the evening, there'll be a dance at the Garage on Kathryn St., with DJ Oli!

So let's get started now, with Matthew!

Matthew Chase-Daniel

GOURDSIGNS

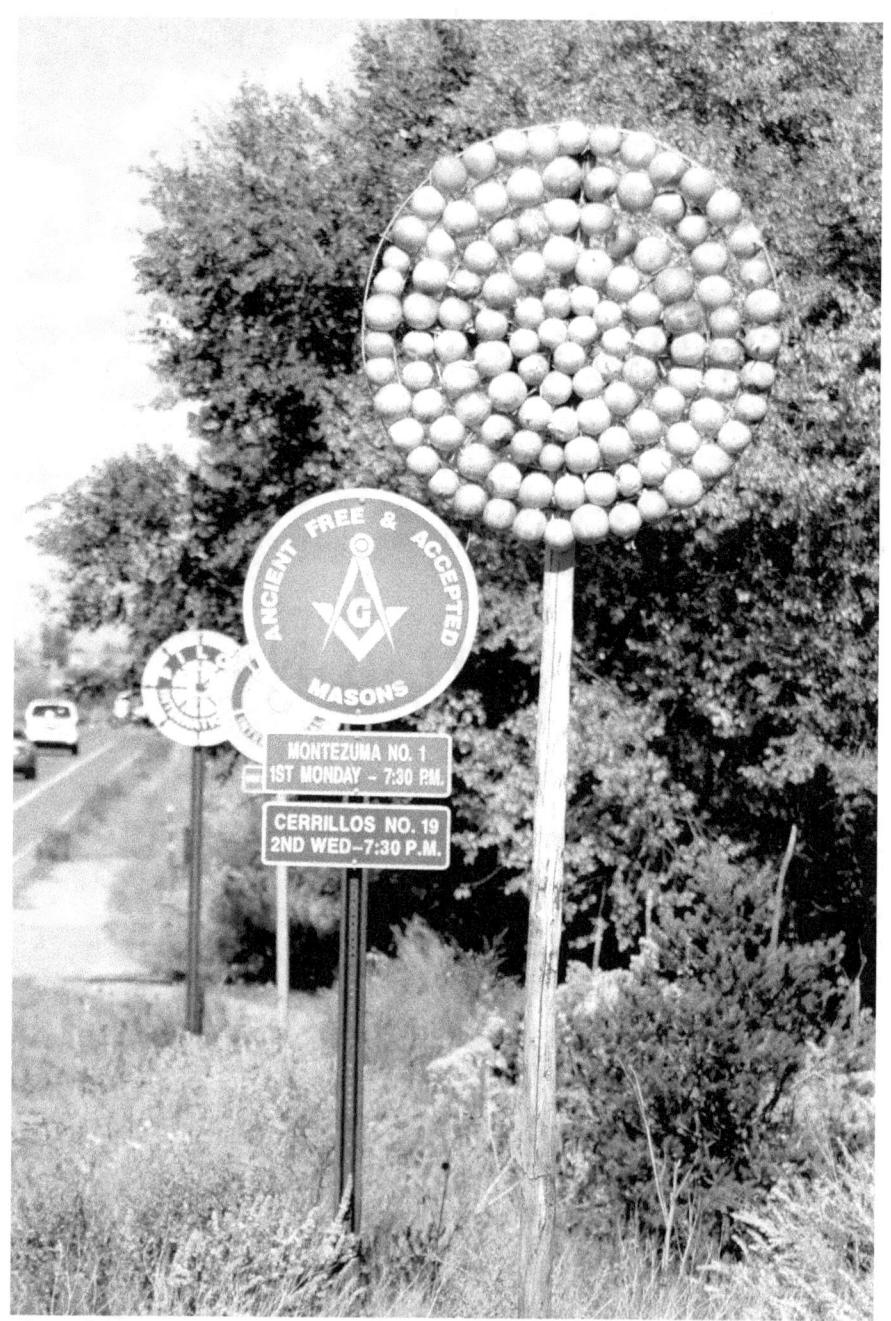

Gourdsign

Matthew Chase-Daniel:

I think I know a lot of you, and I know you mostly through Axle Contemporary, which Jerry Wellman and I run, but I actually exist independently of that as well. So I'm going to talk about a project called Gourdsigns that I did, that started in 2006. Over many years, I put these signs around Santa Fe, near other street signs, in the size of other street signs, but made out of these wild gourds. It started when I first moved to New Mexico; I was fascinated by these gourds, which are called buffalo gourds, or coyote gourds, they grow wild. So I picked a bunch of them -- I had never seen them before -- and strung them up on strings and hung them from a pole. This is a later version but I had done one back in the early nineties, I guess 1990 or so. And this started actually a whole series of different natural materials collected and hung from poles, which I've done in different places round the US and a little in Europe. So anyway, that's a Gourdpole, that was the genesis.

And then, Old Pecos Trail -- from the light up here out to the highway -- was re-paved, and they put in medians and changed the traffic flow there a number of years ago. Part of that was adding these Adopt-a-Median signs, which are little frames about this big. No one had adopted them for a long time and I live out that way, so, I would drive through there a lot and see these empty signs. Because I was bored, driving in my car, I kept thinking about what I should put in there. Or what somebody should put in there. So, I did the first Gourdsign; I stopped one day and measured the opening, built a little wooden frame, strung up a number of gourds in there, and put it up. I didn't get permission from Santa Fe Beautiful (which is the organization that does those), or from the City or the Highway Department. I did an anonymous project, and didn't tell anyone that it was me, until today. [audience laughs] So I hope no one from the police department is here and upset.

Audience Member:

How long did they stay up? Did somebody take them down or did they leave them?

Matthew Chase-Daniel:

Yeah, a combination. Some of them stayed up for three or four years, some of them came down within a day or two. I never knew who, or why they disappeared. Because I didn't want to own it, I couldn't ask questions about it. The first one, and this is on Old Pecos Trail, stayed up for a number of years. Then occasionally -- these gourds don't last too long, they would fall apart; sometimes I would take them down and re-build them and put new ones up. Or the city would put different adopt-a-median signs in new parts of town and I would put one up there. I put one up on St. Francis Drive, kind of near the north side of town, and it was gone in a day. The reason they took that one down was because they had adopted out the median, so they took it down and put up a sign for whoever had paid to adopt the median.

So this was the bus stop at the corner of St. Michael's and Cerrillos, and normally the bus stop signs have this small sign at the bottom and then a tall one that dimension on the top; for some reason on this one the top sign was missing, maybe it was no longer a bus stop, or I'm not sure what. So I measured it and created this frame and hung that one. These ones kind of bulge out on both sides, it's a more dense amount of gourd. And I was always concerned about getting in trouble for doing these, and so I thought maybe I should install them in the middle of the night, when no one was around and no one would see me, but then I thought that if someone did see me, it would look very suspicious. So I just wore sunglasses and a big hat and did them in the middle of the day, and carried the ladder over and made it look like I should be doing it. And no one ever asked me about it.

One day I was riding a little motorized scooter down Old Pecos Trail, this was maybe two or three years ago, and there was this city crew taking one down. And I happened to be turning right there, so I just pulled over by the median in the turn lane, and said, "Oh, are you taking that down?" and they said, "Yes, we leased out the sign", and I said "Oh, well actually I made that, could I have it, if you're just throwing it away?", and he said "Well we usually store them -- we have a whole collection of these at the city, at the maintenance yard, but if it's yours, yeah, of course you can have it." So I just put it between my legs on the scooter and drove off. I don't know if they really do have other ones there or not.

[audience laughs]

So this one is I think thirty inches in diameter, (two and a half feet), and it's the same diameter as these other fraternal organization signs, this is on Old Pecos Trail, just off the freeway, heading towards town. This was up for a few years, and eventually it blew down in a big wind storm, so I took it away. I sort of monitored them -- I was always very concerned not to have them be dangerous for traffic; I put them where there were other signs, in the same places, with the same distance from the road, and all of those sort of things. I tried to conform to the rules, as much as I could understand them.

I find while driving... I live a few miles outside of town, and I come to town most days, so, I see these signs that say "yield" and "speed limit 35" and "stop" and even billboards, and even if I know already what they say, I read them anyway. It gets kind of boring, not very engaging. A lot of us spend a lot of time in our cars, and sometimes we listen to music, or listen to the news or books on tape or whatever. I thought of these Gourdsigns as something visual, something playful, maybe beautiful. And with these repeated objects, something like writing that we have on signs --but not writing with language, just writing with little round balls. So, that's sort of the motivation for that. Here's another picture of that same one. And here's a blurry picture.

This is coming in to town from the north, on St. Francis Drive; it's the size of a speed limit sign. It disappeared within a day or two. I have no idea why. And here's a close-up of that one. They start off green, they dry into that kind of yellowish color, and then they go this sort of golden tan. Then, when you harvest them, and when you string them up and dry them out, sometimes they rot really badly and turn into mush, and other times they get these hard shells that last for a really long time. And I haven't totally figured out what the variables are.

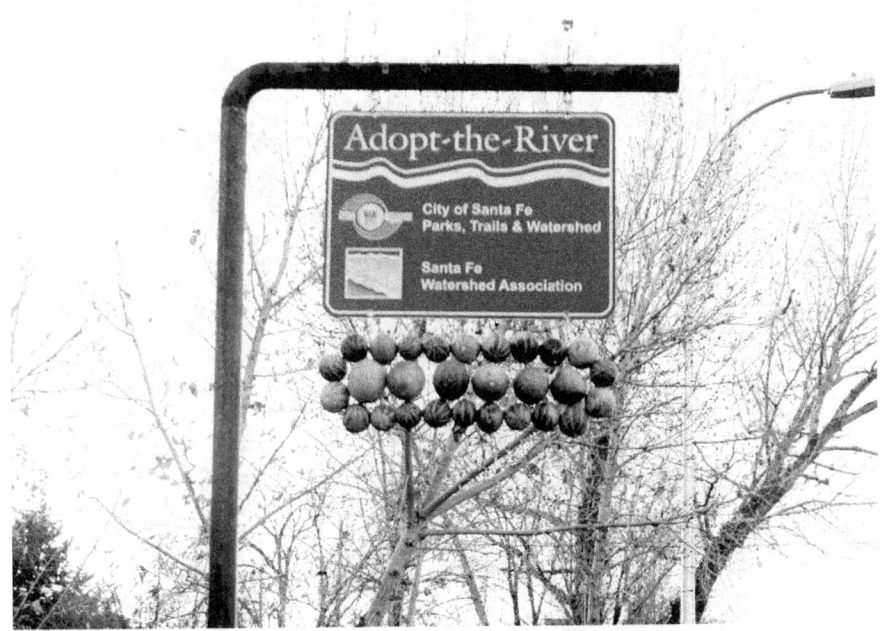

Gourdsign

This is on Old Santa Fe Trail, behind Quail Run, kind of heading out of town towards Cañada de Los Alamos. It's curve signs. And this is an "Adopt a River" that also disappeared fairly quickly, that's down on Alameda.

This one is still there. There was this sign post with that bar coming out, it must have used to have been the sign of a business, it was maybe Noon Whistle Cafe and then Aqua Santa, and now it's Bouche, but it's the back of the building, on Alameda downtown. So I just put it up there, climbed up on the wall with the ladder, didn't ask, but I guess they didn't mind, cause it's still there. And this one for some reason had dried out and stayed pretty solid, I think it's the only one that is still up. So I started in 2006, and I don't know when the last one I put up was, maybe 2010?

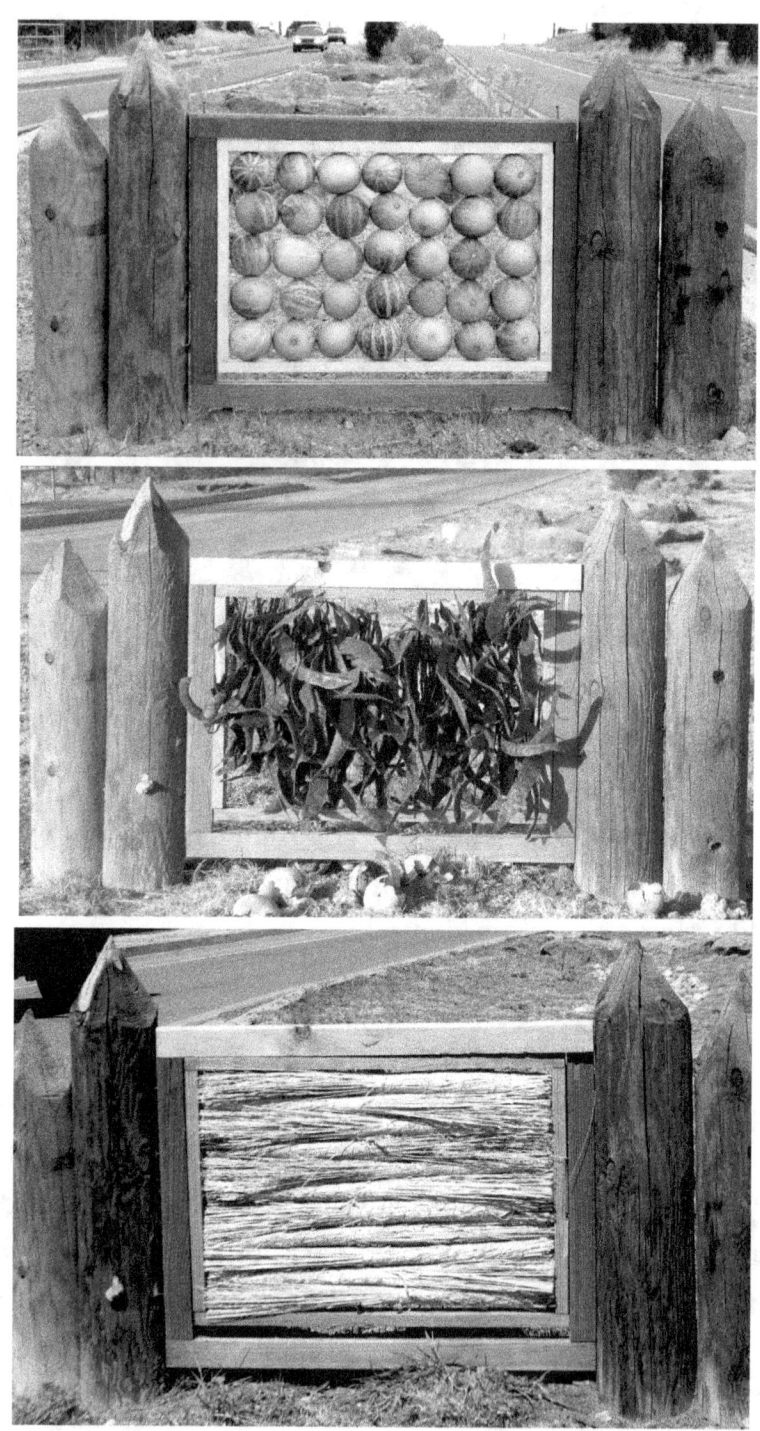

Gourdsigns

That was another empty sign, the top part of that post was empty and some sign that had been there had come down, it's near Dunkin Donuts on St. Francis... here's the same one. This... I had a show of some of my other drawings and sculptures at the New Mexico Museum of Art, one of the Alcove shows a year or two ago. So the day of the show -- there's this little hole in the building that didn't go to anything, just this sort of recess -- so I walked around and found that hole, and made this little sort of waterfall coming out of there. It disappeared within a day, I didn't tell the museum that it was mine...

And a couple of them, I experimented using other things. So these were bundles of grasses, of Side Oats Gramma, which is a native grass. And these are seed pods from a Locust tree, that I collected downtown, on Palace Avenue -- that's also on Old Pecos Trail, you can see remnants of gourds from what was there before -- I had taken one down that rotted away.

Audience Member:

Did those last as long, the grasses and seedpod ones?

Matthew Chase Daniel:

The grasses one lasted a long time, and the seedpod one somebody came and broke it -- stamped on it, I don't know what they did. So I found it broken, a couple of weeks later. When you're doing these anonymous, unsanctioned things, you have very little control over security. It's an interesting thing, because, I wanted them to be anonymous when I did them, but I also, as an artist, have this desire to have credit for what I've done, and to document them.

So it's this interesting balance, and that's some of what we're talking about today, these ephemeral, temporary things... how do you get funding, how do you get credit, how do you get documentation. In the beginning, it was just 'cause I wanted to do this, and I didn't want to get in trouble, so I was like ok, I'll be anonymous and I'll do it -- I didn't have a plan to do a series of them, I just did one, and then I saw another and decided to do another. And it's not meant to have some big social implications or anything, this project is just very playful, just to give people a little visual something to play with during their day. I think that's the end of the slides.

Audience Member:

So, first, it isn't exactly a social thing, but for me, when I've seen them -- and before I met you, I saw them -- there's that thing of, you've taken a street sign, and you've put this object that we see in nature (in northern New Mexico, we see those, they're everywhere) and so for me, there's humor involved, which I love, but there's also that aspect of putting something from the wild into a place that normally has a sign that nobody ever reads... my question is though, you string them, like beads?

Matthew Chase Daniel:

Yeah, I use waxed nylon, you can get it at Tandy Leather, and I poke holes; I made a big sort of sewing needle, and I poke a hole going through them, going both this way and that way, so they're fairly solid in the frame. That lighter-colored frame, I built out of wood and screwed and glued it together, and then I drilled holes, at the center of each gourd, so the thread comes through here and then to the outside of the frame. And then I took that frame and just screwed it with deck screws into the existing frame that they had. So some are done that way, others... this one, the frame is made out of steel wire that's soldered together with silver solder to make a structural frame, and then the gourds are tied onto that with the same kind of thing and then that whole thing is attached to a post. So some are done that way.

Audience Member:

Thank you, I love them.

Audience Member:

This is really cool to happen to be here -- these have totally fascinated me, ever since they started, and whenever people come into town that are visiting, I'll take them on a tour of where I think these signs are... the one on Alameda is always there... But it's been really inspirational, really cool, it's a great project.

I have a couple of questions though, and one is, now that it's revealed that it's you, do you stop, or does the project continue?

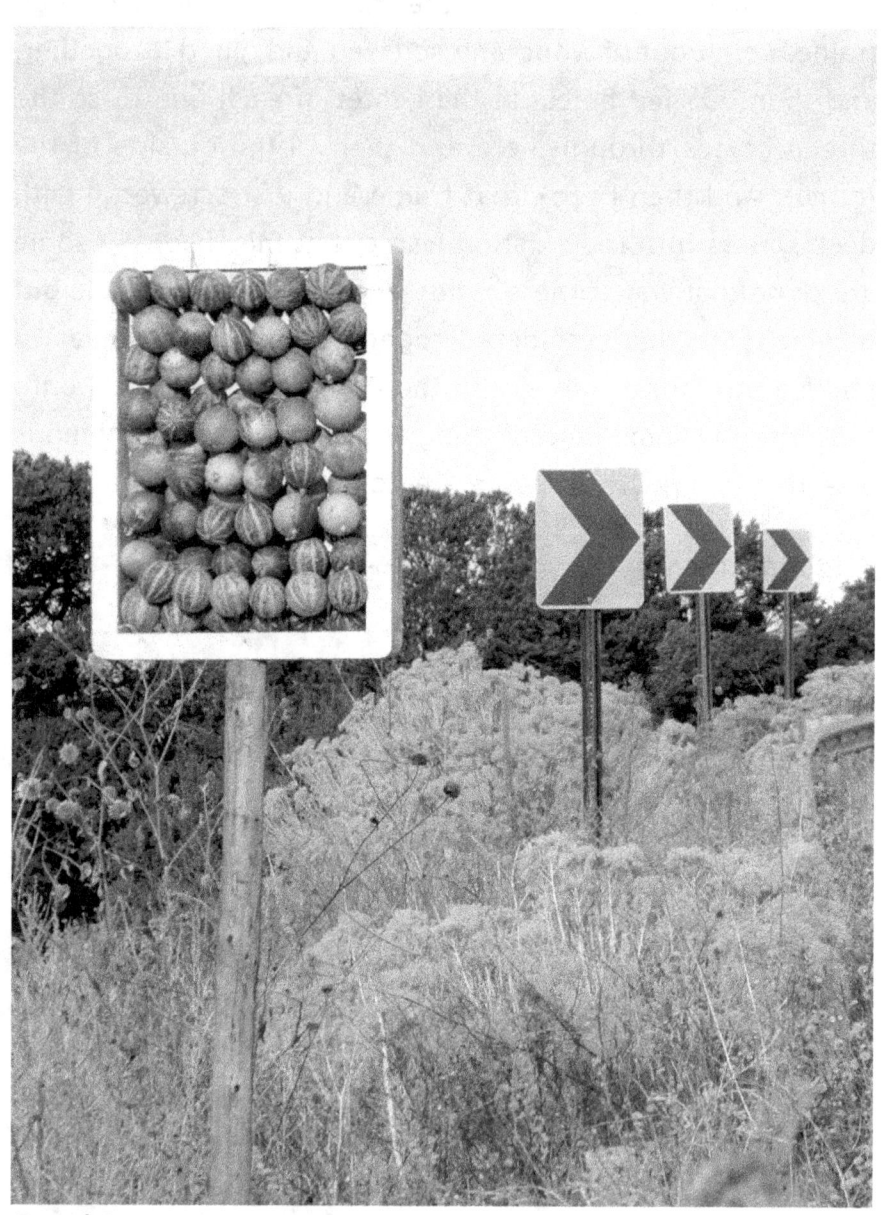

Gourdsign

Matthew Chase-Daniel:

I don't know, good question. I haven't done any for a few years, and it's probably just because I've been busy, doing other projects, running Axle, doing other things. And it's a pretty time-consuming project. You know, I don't get the sense that the City or the Highway Department or any of those organizations is out to get me, so I might be able to do more. But yeah, it's a little tricky that way, the balance between doing it anonymously and having credit or being known...maybe I do more, or maybe I do other projects that are different enough that it's not an issue. The Gourdpoles, and the other poles, which are related, I've done a lot of those and have always taken credit for those. Those to me are more something that I can continue to do that's related. I've applied actually for certain public art commissions in other cities to do Gourdsigns, and sent them my photos and said, I did this in Santa Fe, and I'd like to do it in... I've never gotten any of those commissions...

Audience Member:

So my second question is, in the process of doing this, how important was the rogue nature, for you?

Matthew Chase-Daniel:

I don't know, that's hard to answer. If I had put a little plaque on the bottom of each one, so if someone pulled over and looked, they could figure out who it was -- that would have been okay with me. That wouldn't have diminished it, because it's mostly for everyone who's driving by... so the anonymity, or the illegality or the rogue nature, isn't that important. It was just, I guess maybe a lot easier, than to try and get permission. I didn't think I would be able to get permission. There are other projects, where that rogue, anonymous aspect maybe is more important. I was also very careful, with these, not to do anything that was dangerous or destructive, because I think there's a lot of graffiti art and anonymous art where, some of it I find really engaging and great, and some of it I find destructive...If you do graffiti and even if it's a beautiful thing, and it's on someone's building who owns it and doesn't want that, that's problematic. I really enjoy these unauthorized rogue projects but, we all need to be really careful to do them responsibly. Maybe we can take one more question.

Audience Member:

First I want to say that I also, from the first time I saw this project, was just so tickled -- I don't know how many other people had that same feeling, but it just made me feel happy. I was wondering, if you were to do this project now, with all the experience you've had with these Gourdsigns and running Axle and other projects you've been doing, is there anything you would do differently?

Matthew Chase-Daniel:

No. I mean I feel like now that I run Axle I have a very public face, and some sort of responsibility to behave responsibly, so going out to do something that's borderline illegal, is a little more irresponsible than in 2006, when most people didn't know who I was, so it's a little different. I'm doing another project now which ends tomorrow; it's the last day. On Kickstarter I raised fifteen hundred dollars with Axle, for this thing called "Dollar Distribution." I have fifteen hundred dollar bills, and each day for a month, I'm putting fifty individual dollar bills in different places around the city, mostly just dropped on the sidewalk, but sometimes in the crack in the side of a tree, or a book in the library, and things like that. And that is also sort of borderline anonymous -- I mean I'm publicizing it, and trying to get as much awareness about it as possible, and taking photos of some of the dollar bills in their little spots, and putting them on the internet. But I also want most people who find them to not know it's a project -- they're not marked, there's nothing written on them -- to just have that engaging experience of finding money on the street; fifteen hundred different people having that experience, and having it be what it is... without reference to some conceptual framework around it. And that's again a tricky thing; as an artist I want credit for it, I want publicity for it. But for the project, I want it to be anonymous. So, I want everyone to know about it except the fifteen hundred people who find the dollar bills, and that's kind of tricky. [audience laughs]

Audience Member:

Thank you. My name is Issa, I just wanted to acknowledge your work because you're one of the artists that I follow here in town, and I think through this work, you're trying to tell the community that you like this town, and this is your contribution. You don't have to wait for funding or to get any public commission to love Santa Fe. So that's the way I see it, but my question for you is, do you have a title for them?

Matthew Chase-Daniel: I call them Gourdsigns.

Audience Member: I mean each piece.

Matthew Chase-Daniel:

No, not so much. I call them "adopt a median sign" and "curve sign" and "speed limit sign", and "bus stop sign," but that's more for my own reference, they're pretty much untitled.

Audience Member:

I see generosity of spirit throughout your work. And within the context of that generosity of spirit, I think had you overly advertised the fact that it was yours, some of that generosity of spirit would be diminished. I also think that dancing with the legality and illegality of your project, creates another situation in which to address that generosity of spirit, and how odd it is that doing something generous like this might be illegal. I find that to be interesting as well. So the question of the rogueness or illegality or the anonymity -- perhaps you didn't think of it but it doesn't really matter -- it causes us to have to think about those kinds of issues, especially in relation to public art, and what public art is becoming more and more today, which is -- the value and the response that you get is oftentimes very indirect. Anyway, I just want to salute you for this work.

Matthew Chase-Daniel:

Thank you, yeah it sounds like what you're saying and Issa's saying as well, is there's a generosity and it's a gift to Santa Fe, as a place I care about, to do this and put it out there for other people. And I think that's true, I like that take on it.

Audience Member:

Matthew, just picking up on what Jerry said, I feel the same way -- I think of you as kind of a pollinator of imagination. And I think those of us involved in public art, very involved in structures and institutions and that kind of thing, I feel like you're holding a very very critical space, here in Santa Fe, so I want to just look at you and say thank you for that, and may we continue to support you.

Matthew Chase-Daniel:

Thanks. it's a tricky balance, because this project took a lot of time, and there's no payment for it. For the Dollar Distribution project, I raised fifteen hundred dollars, and I give away fifteen hundred dollars, and it's a lot of work. It has changed my relationship to money -- every day, for the last month, I leave the house with fifty one-dollar bills, and rather than -- you all look at that and think 'wow, that's a lot of money' -- rather than it being something of value to me, like "oh, I could get a cappuccino and a croissant." I'm like 'Damn, that's a lot of work that I still have to do today! [audience laughs] "It's already ten o'clock and I've barely even started…" It's a very strange thing.

So that's an interesting question in terms of institutions of public art, and projects like these that are not sanctioned and not balanced, and how can can we continue to do things like this and support them. Axle Contemporary is having our annual fund drive, so if you want to give us any money, [audience laughs] we support things like that...

Audience Member:

Hi, it's Michelle. I live out that way too, and I saw those every day. And although in listening to you I hear you say that the rogue-ness and guerilla-ness weren't important to you, they were to me, as the viewer. And I feel like I had a different experience coming across them daily and wondering... just knowing that they weren't a 'sanctioned' public art project. That somebody was doing that, somebody was popping these up, for me, to see on my way in. And I'd see different ones... And working in the institutional public art world as I do now, and wanting to fund projects like this -- at the same time, thinking about it while you were talking, as a viewer, it would have wrecked it. So it's sort of a weird dynamic, I don't know how we work with that.

Matthew Chase-Daniel:

Yes. a Catch 22. Thanks, one more question.

Audience Member:

Hi, I love this, and I think we'll get into this more as we listen to the projects, but it made me think about permission, did they get permission to do this? And just that whole idea of asking permission to make art. It comes into public art, because sometimes it's on someone's property... So I'm curious how that comes up, how that's handled also in the other projects. Because also by asking permission, in some way you're asking for restrictions.

Matthew Chase-Daniel:

Yeah. At Axle Contemporary we did this project called Haiku Roadsign in 2011. It was this portable sign with plastic letters, and we had thirty-two haiku on it. We moved it to a different visible location each week for three months or something -- 16 weeks, four months. We got permission from all the property owners, and they were all visible from the street. There was a U-Haul dealer, and a museum, you know, a whole range of places. But it still had that aspect of surprise, when you went by, and you weren't expecting to see a poem on one of these cheesy signs. So I think there are ways to get permission and still have it have that unexpected charm. But for these Gourdsigns, it would have been impossible -- especially as at that time, I was not as well known. Like now, I know the people at the Santa Fe Arts Commission, and New Mexico Arts. But to try and get permission, probably still, with the highway right of way... it's a tricky thing. There it's another un-sanctioned public art project on Old Pecos Trail: Someone has been throwing shoes in the median, for, I don't know, fifteen, twenty years. And I don't know who that is, I've heard rumors it might be Carlos Glass. I'm not sure if that's true. It just goes on and on, and there's been articles in the paper about it maybe fifteen years ago -- that's an interesting project, I'm not sure what it's supposed to mean.

It's not quite as beautiful necessarily as a sign or something, it's more subtle, but it's interesting, and it's on-going -- and maybe it's different people who are taking it up...

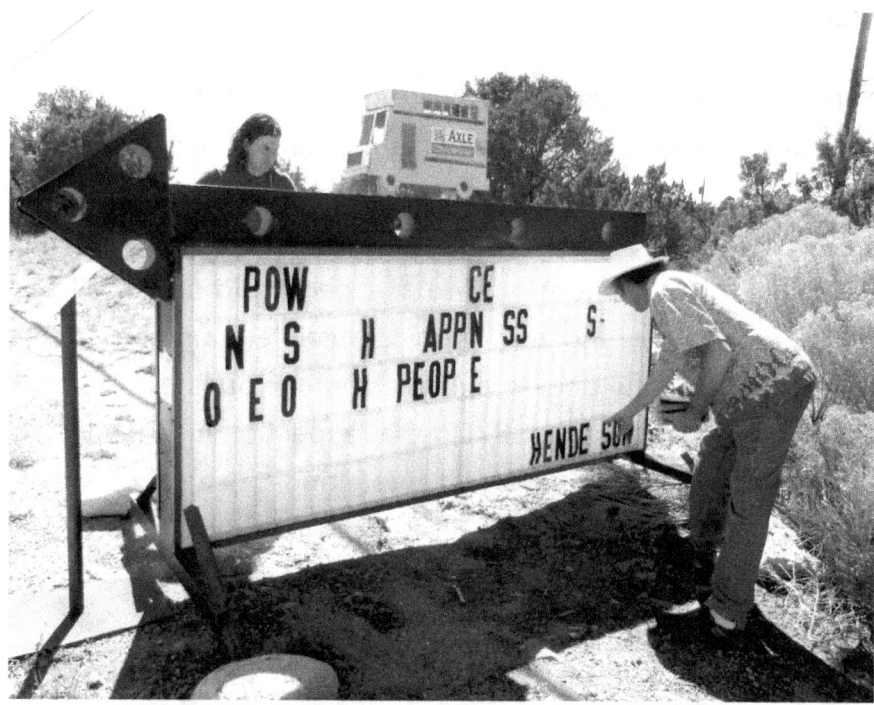

Axle Contemporary: *Haiku Roadsign*

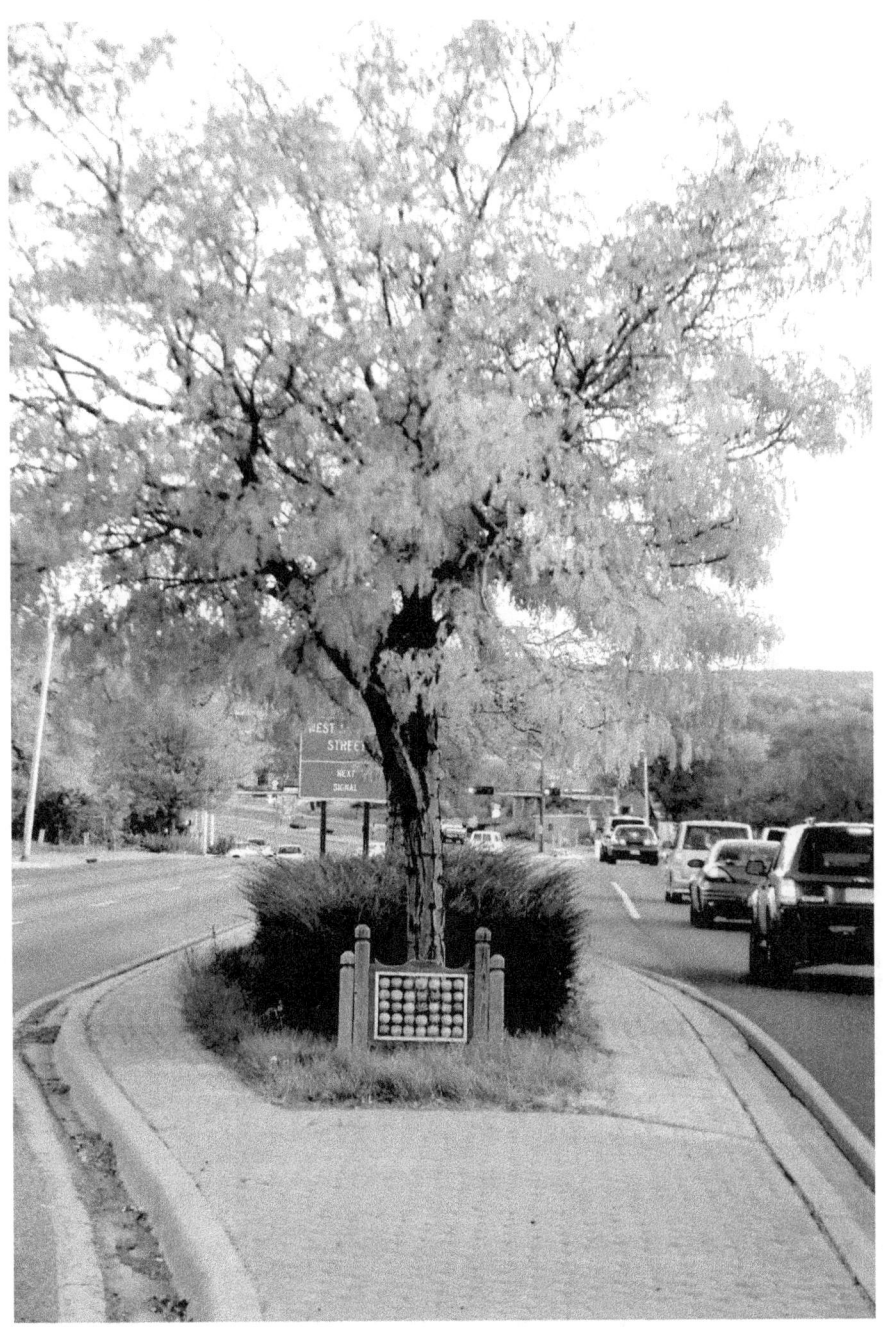

Gourdsign

Aly Kreikemeier

EL OTRO LADO

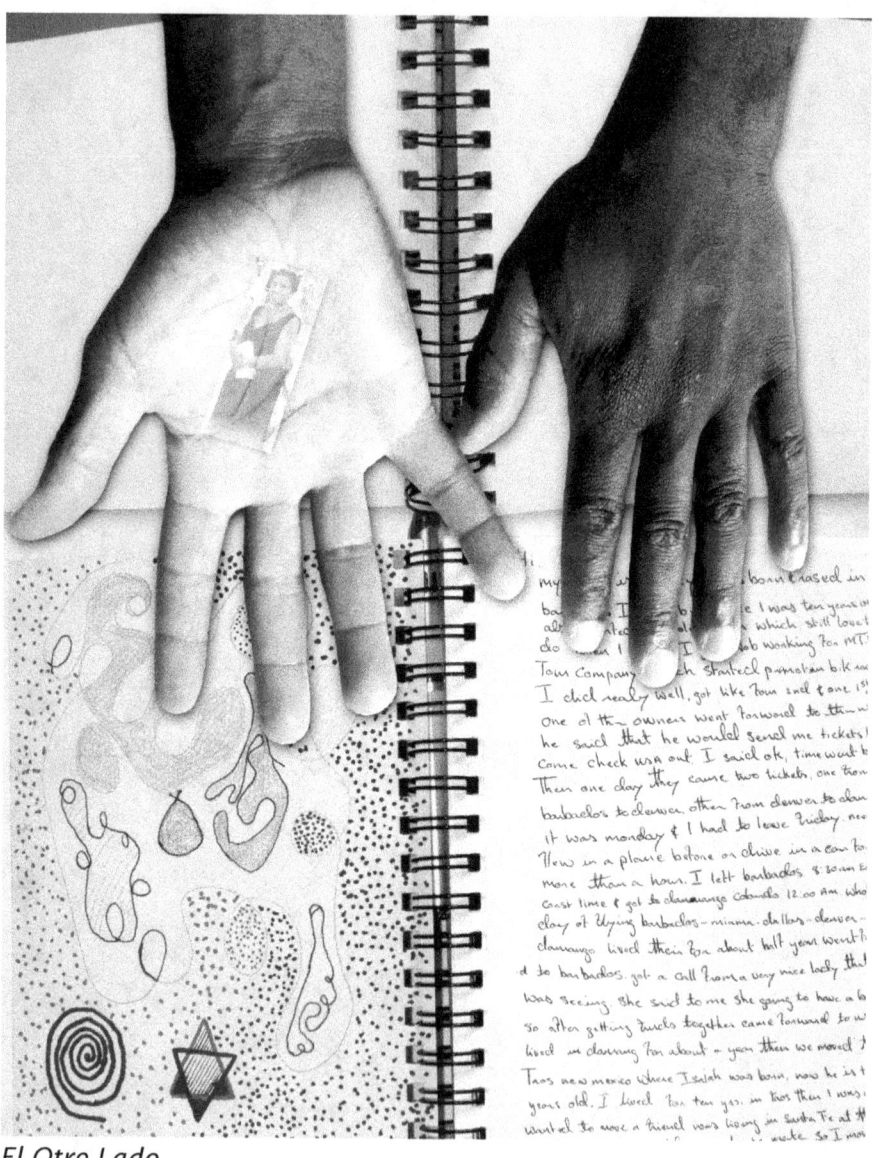

El Otro Lado

38

Aly Kreikemeier:

Good Morning everyone, my name is Aly, and I manage the El Otro Lado Schools Program.

I just want to start with a really brief introduction of where the project has come from; then we have about a ten minute video that does a really beautiful job of showing what this actually looks like in the schools, as well as giving the opportunity to let some of the teaching artists and teachers and the founder, Chrissie Orr, speak to the program for themselves. I'll close with a little bit of reflection and learning that we have observed over the last four years now since we've been in the schools.

El Otro Lado actually began, some of you may remember, in 2007/2008, when community artist Chrissie Orr was working with The Santa Fe Art Institute around the question of migration, borders and identity. So the project really seeks to use the multi-disciplinary creative process to explore our connection to land, our sense of belonging at home, and our connection in the sense of cultural boundary.

It began with these multimedia workshops, over the course of one or two years, that Chrissie helped run all throughout Santa Fe. Then she pulled together different stories and images, and they went up on big panels around the city in 2008 and 2009 in Santa Fe. The project then went on further to do a similar thing-- a little bit bigger, in Albuquerque, working closely with Michelle Otero and several other artists, in the senior center and schools in Albuquerque.

So it was a very cross-cultural, inter-generational group of people pulling together their own stories, and using the creative process to look at "Who are we here?" and "How do we see one another?"

So that project in Albuquerque was 2009/2010, and since then we've been in the Santa Fe Public Schools, which is a little bit of a different turn. It's been a really interesting evolution, I think, for the program.

It's a program of the Academy for the Love of Learning, and you'll hear more about that with Lifesongs, I believe this morning. Chrissie was facilitating a group of teachers -- the Academy works with a lot of teachers -- and using the creative experience to go into teachers stories of who they are and why they teach, and kind of get back to the heart of learning. And they were just like, "this is amazing! We have to bring this to our classrooms." So it opened this next phase of collaboration that turned the work, these workshops and this use of the creative process, into something like a curriculum. I kind of hate that word and am taking it out of the next guide. Essentially, there was a guide produced of all of these different art experiences surrounding journaling and surrounding the visual arts, and then we bring that curriculum in with teaching artists to the Santa Fe Public schools. That kicked off in 2010/2011. That was the first year.

It's been interesting. I've realized, reflecting on how to carry this story forward to someone who's come on since it's been in the schools and who wasn't a part of the original project. I realized, that in some ways, the way that Chrissie really facilitated and saw these workshops in the community, and used the creative process and then harvested the stories and the things that came from that in a sort of public witnessing, is what's happening in sort of a microcosm in each classroom and with each teaching artist.

So I think that's a really key piece of the program when you're working with the public schools and working in an institution. The question of how do we avoid this becoming just a program, coming from the top down? In many ways lives in the aliveness of having an artist in the classroom working with teachers, running these workshops.

I think that's all I'll say in terms of the introduction and the video will give a really nice portion of what this actually is.

So we produced this video last spring, and it's sort of a culmination of different footage over the last three years in the schools.

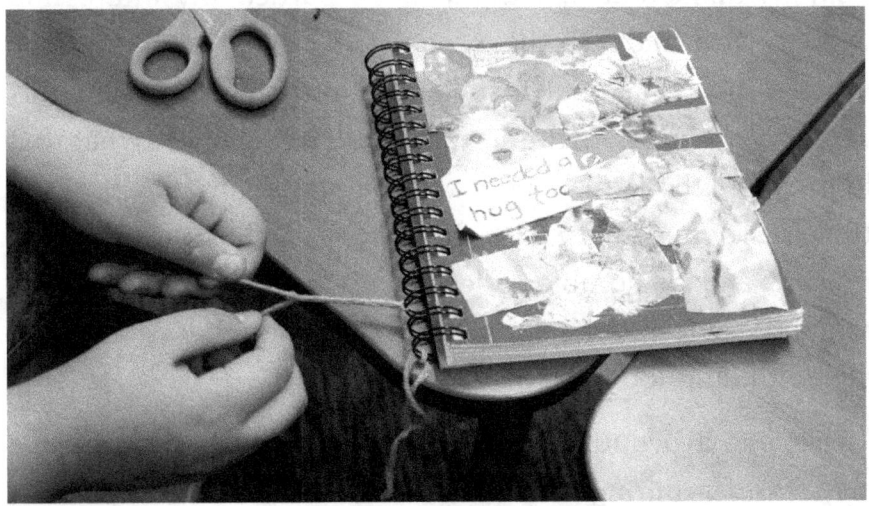

El Otro Lado

[video] See video at www.evolvingintentionsinpublicart.org

I love that film, and I have to say that before coming on here

I taught at a middle school in town, and when I first saw the film, I was blown away to see some of my former students and these sides of them through this film that I never saw in the classroom. I think that's really the power of the work; the way in which bringing in the creative process allows students and teachers to go into themselves, in a different way and in a deeper way.

So much of the heart of this work is really around relationship. You saw that in the way that the teacher and teaching artist talk about how they work together, and the new way that they grow to see their students through the stories that are shared.

In a few closing comments, I'd like to speak a little bit about the growing pains and what we've learned and where we're going. I think that one thing that's particularly interesting with El Orto Lado in the schools, is having come from a more public art initial installation, and then bringing this very much into an institution. How do we navigate what that looks like? I think in a lot of ways the process that happens in the classroom -- this way of working -- is all about using the process and being able to let go of what your expectations might be and what the end of a session might be: What a self-portrait might look like or not.

There was a beautiful story a woman shared of creating a clay shrine; during the program she made this perfect, immaculate shrine, and it meant so much to her, and it shattered. Throughout the project she came back and by the end of the culminating event, she had this mosaic. The way in which something that she was really working on and really attached to and had vision for, shattered, and she had to find a new way. I think is really a great metaphor for how this works.

So we see that in the classroom. But then in terms of actually leading the program, and looking at where do we go with the program, how does it grow, who do we work with, and how do we navigate all of these different facets -- I think that's also very process-oriented.

I just wanted to speak to that briefly, to think about how we are holding a clear artistic intention of where this work is going. What this work is, and what it is not. Which is particularly interesting to hold onto when you're working in the public schools, and when there are so many programs that become codified and institutionalized into something else that teachers do in their classroom. How do we ensure that this is a little bit more alive and moving. So one piece of that is really that navigating, having a clear intention and holding onto that, and then, listening. Just as relationship is at the heart of this, so is deep listening.

This sort of work takes time, and it's about being able to build relationships with teachers, and with schools; in the same way that the teachers and students really build a deeper relationship through the work in the classroom, we're doing that at the program level.

It's challenging to really listen and hear what's being needed and what's being asked for, and to feel out where the program wants to go, and then to reconcile how that fits or doesn't fit with the intention that we hold for the program. I think that's a really interesting piece to hold with the public schools.

I was just recalling this morning, I was meeting with a principal over the summer, talking about where we're going this year at one of the schools that we've been involved with the longest. He was so thrilled about the program, which is fabulous because we of course need administrative support. But then we also have to really hold that we're listening to the teachers, and that this program is really supporting the teachers in the schools. The public schools can be a pretty rough place at the moment, actually, and are just becoming more and more standardized. So how do we hold a teacher's unique vision, and who they are in the classroom, when we're thinking about where to go with this work?

So, I had this meeting with the principal and a teacher, and we were talking about the vision for the program in their school for the year, and he was not only thrilled about the work, he was like, "we'll give you whatever meetings you want, we can do open houses..." he was so open to deepening El Otro Lado in the schools, and deepening the way we engage the community. Then he said something that really startled me, both with excitement and with a little bit of caution. He said, you know, it won't be a problem convincing people because we have the highest English language arts scores in 5th grade, which is the grade which this program is in. It was like 75%. When I was working in the public schools, the school I was at was maybe 20%. Especially in the public schools with so many English language learners this is huge. So the principal was so thrilled that we have this data that he was able to at least nominally link to El Otro Lado, because it was the only thing that was particularly different about this grade. So with that, there is this excitement -- that we can see the ways this work is rippling out in unintended consequences and enriching other areas of these students lives, academically as well. But it also made me wonder: -- Wow, how do we hold this data driven angle, how do we ensure that this doesn't become a defining feature or become some sort of boundary as to where the program goes or why it goes a certain way?

With that, I will close out by saying that, in terms of navigating that balance, I do feel that relationship and deep listening, while holding onto intention, is how we're able to really navigate it. I just want to read some little phrases of the intention of the program, which actually is both what we hold that this work would do in the schools (with our students, with our teachers in the community), and also what we've witnessed. So it's kind of sweet when you see your intentions and outlooks align.

So that's all I have. I don't know if there are any questions, we have a few minutes.

> EOL is responsive to cultural values.
>
> It is activating learning through using the creative process, through both personal and collective story.
>
> Bringing empathy into the classroom.
>
> Encouraging teachers to be authentic and to practice learning alongside their students.
>
> Supporting teachers and teaching artists to partner in their listening.
>
> EOL values difference and the EOL creates a sense of belonging.

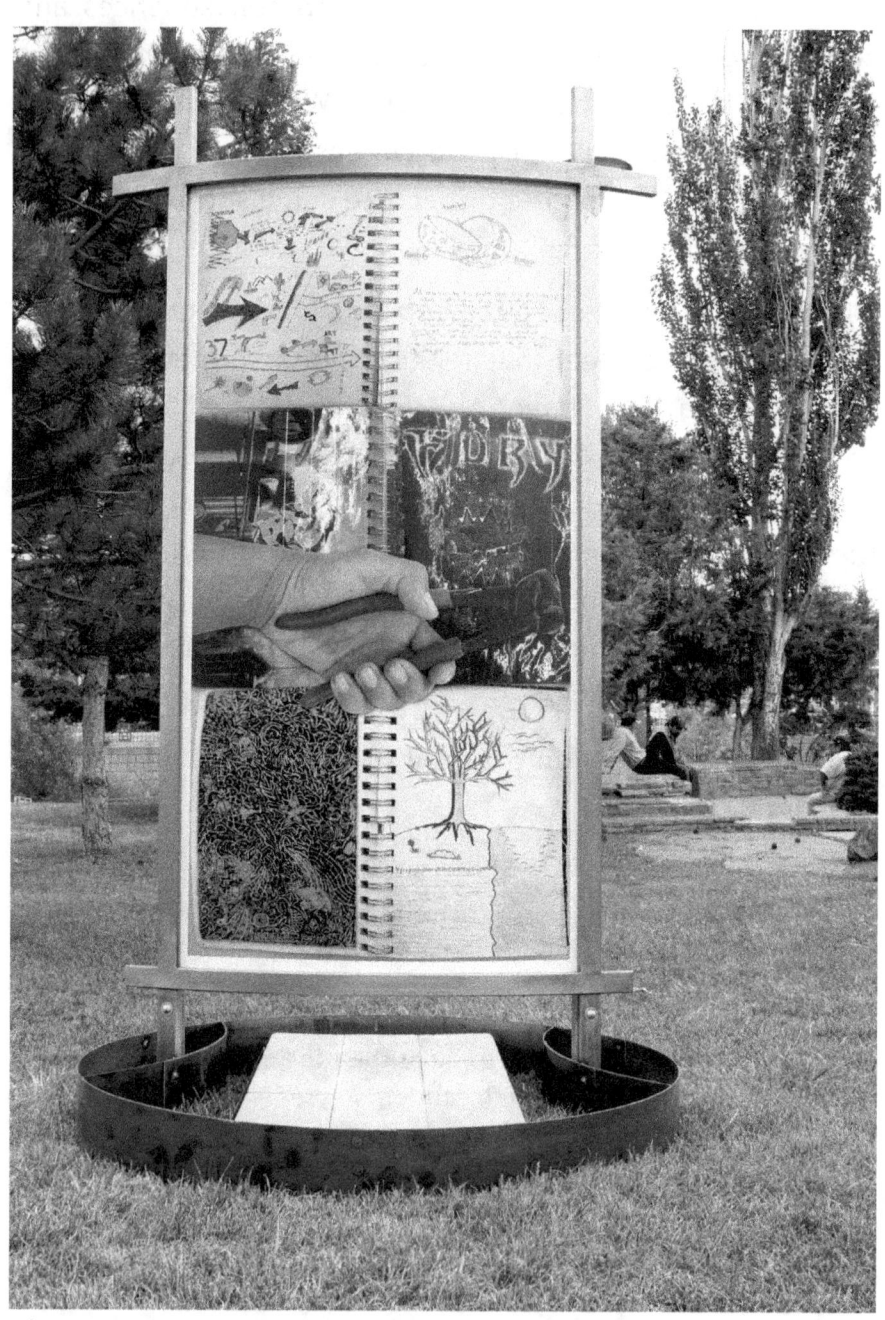

El Otro Lado

46

Audience Member:

You spoke a little bit about quantifications in the schools. I guess you're saying that you have quantifiable results, helpful, but it's also not your aim to meet those results, you have different aims. So before you had these quantifiable results, did you find it a challenge to find a time and a curriculum, from the teacher to the administration, to do a project that's aim is not to see those results?

My other question is the funding. Does funding come from the public schools, or from the Academy for the Love of Learning?

Aly Kreikemeier:

Thank you. To the first one -- we've had qualitative impact all along. That's been very clear because so much of the work is documented. So it's photographing, it's speaking with students, it's speaking with teachers. At the end of each year they have these events that are community-wide and really share the impact that the programs have. So I think from the beginning we've had very qualitative, but not so much quantitative. And as that starts to emerge, we're holding-- What is our relationship to quantitative data? We're just stepping into that boat. The qualitative data has been there from the beginning, having come from the work that began as a public installation. The whole project came from the request of teachers, having seen the power themselves of this work and saying- this would be incredible for my students.

The funding ties into that in a trippy way. A good portion of the funding comes from the Academy for the Love of

Learning. We have had grants in the past, and we have had some funding come through the schools, which has been a really beautiful gift and supported our teaching artists and the materials. We bring materials into the public schools as well as teaching artists in this curriculum.

We did a crowd-funding campaign recently that raised money to support a teaching artist for a whole year. That was the first time like that and was really exciting. So we are diversifying our funding streams to some extent. The piece that's the most interesting for me about this, is where the public schools come into play -- that collaborative piece, making sure this is a collaboration. Also being wary, although, I have to say that the funding that we've had in the past has been generous and has worked beautifully.

What I'm learning surprisingly, given the state of our public schools, is there is actually a lot of untapped funding available at the administrative level. So we have sat with that. How can we tap into that, but also, do we want to? We have had some in the past, but again, I hold that question -- sitting with one foot in the institution of the public schools and one foot out -- we just have to be very intentional about what receiving funding from the public schools might mean, in terms of the expectations of the program.

Thank you so much!

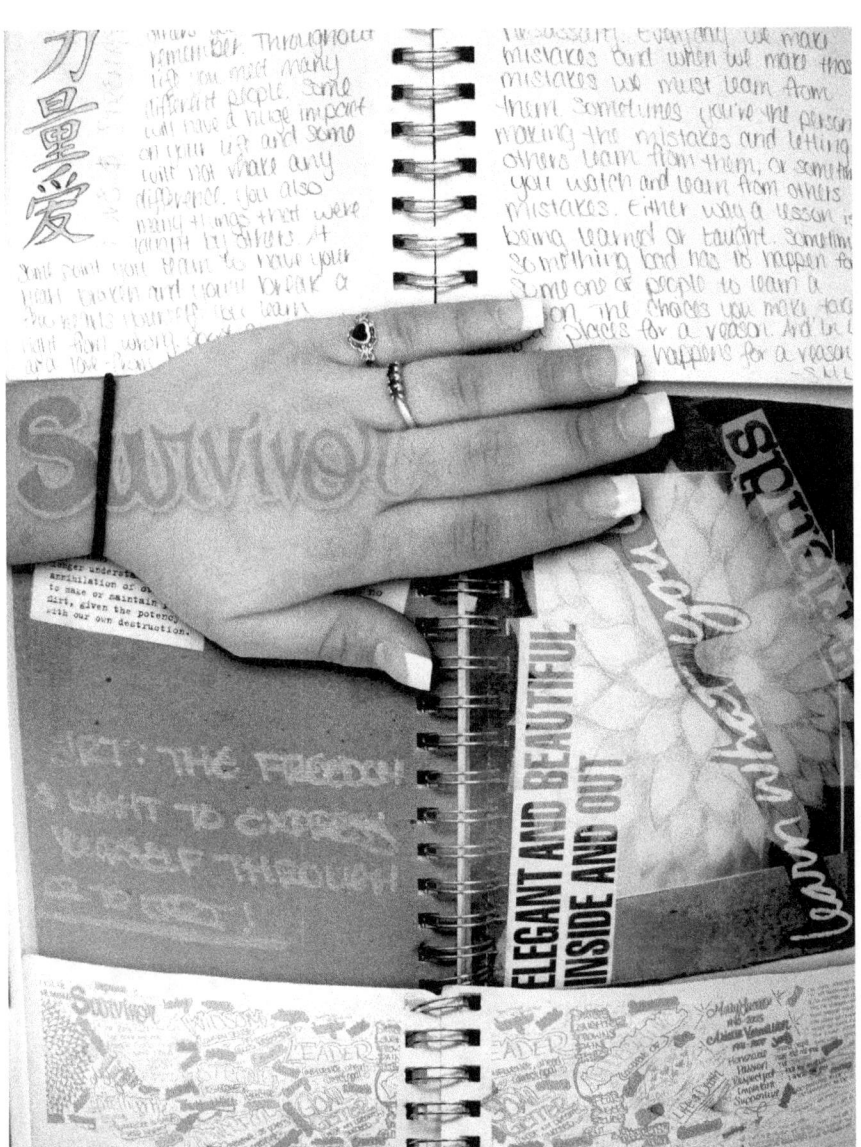

El Otro Lado

Molly Sturges

LIFESONGS

COAL

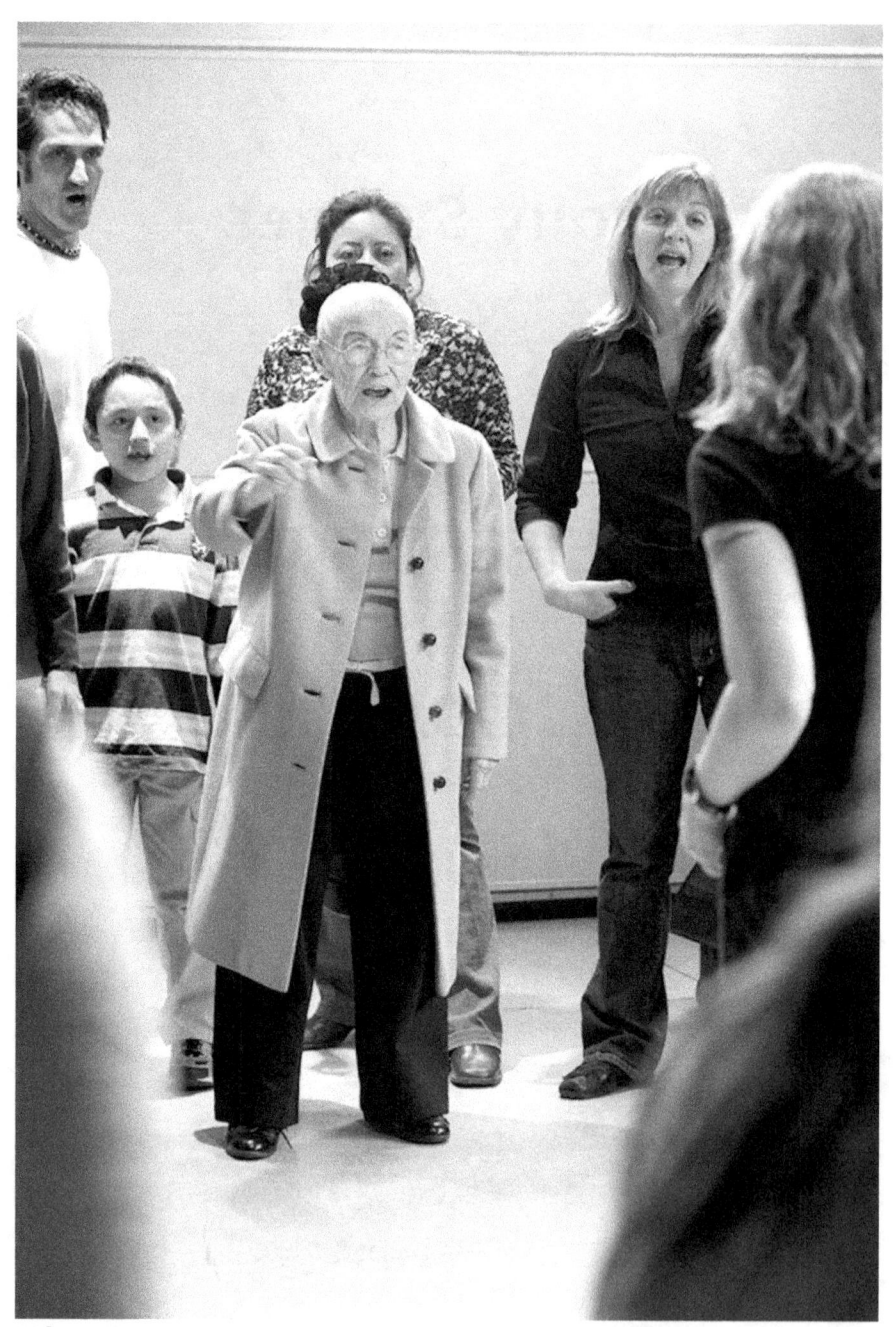

Lifesongs

Molly Sturges:

I just wanted to start with a little bit of music. It's always a good thing, and I'll try to end with some music as well.

I just want to say a big huge thank you to this woman right here. There's nothing easy about organizing an event like this, as we all know, and thanks to Christy and thanks to everybody for being here. It's really rare for me to get to sit with my colleagues, and listen to them speak about their work. I know that everybody in here is thinking about and doing incredible things, and I look forward to the time when we can have more time together, and continue this really important kind of dialogue. It happens so rarely. I know in this town and community there's just so much vitality. So may we continue to catalyze it, and learn with each other, so we get better and better at doing it.

So, I drank a lot of coffee. I don't drink coffee very often so I wish we could just like run around while we talk. [laughter]

I wanted to start today with a story -- looking at my colleague here, Alysha Shaw who does Lifesongs with me -- last night we were performing some of the songs and stories of Lifesongs. So I'm going to open today with a story and a song. But before I do that I just want to give you a little context for this moment.

I have been doing community -- what I call community sourced artwork -- for about eighteen years. I probably started a lot earlier; I used to go to nursing homes with my grandma, who was an amazing pianist and we would sit there and I just fell in love with what happened when she started playing music. And you know as a choir nerd, it was always kind of weird to go to a nursing home because it smells, and it's depressing, and all that stuff. But something about my grandmother's love of doing that, I bring to you today. Her name is Edie, and it's always the source that I go back to.

So I come to you as an experimental musician -- that was my love, and I love improvisational structures and trying out new things. When I was in graduate school, I got really super fed up because I'd have these concerts, and it was always the same twenty five people. Every time it was like, the experimental music nerds, right? And it was super exciting for us, as a little group of artist-scientists, but I really had some problems, because I had also come out of a background of activism and facilitation, and I didn't quite know how to join those worlds.

So I came out of graduate school and I thought, well, I'll just try something. So I went to this cancer center. Even before I had gotten out of graduate school, I started saying in my composition classes "yeah, I'm going to compose for some people at a cancer center." And they were like, "Oh yeah, the pieces are about cancer." And I was like, "no actually, they're not about cancer." But, you know, it started me working in this way that was very relational, and it's nothing new, really. We're talking about an old human practice of having art that helps us navigate really challenging things in life. Art that helps us realign, when our identity and our sense of self and our expressiveness is capped, and we don't know how to enliven ourselves in life. This is what humans have been doing for a long time, and artists in the west -- certainly there is a long history of this.

So I just kind of found myself there by interest, and I started working in the cancer center as a composer, it was amazing. I was super confused because all my colleagues -- experimental composers -- were like, "Oh, that's so sweet." (wreeaghh). Do you know what I'm saying? Yeah. The minute that you start working with people, it's like "Oh that's so sweet" and "Oh you're helping those people," and I was like, "I don't know, I think I might be helping myself more than anybody." right? We've got this a little bit mixed up. This is pretty mixed up. It's like a colonization in the brain or something.

So I started working, and I was like, "Wow, wait a second!" I was doing this duet with a woman who had stage four cancer. She was from the Ukraine. She had no family and we did this little score that could have been a John Cage score. From one side of the room to the other, there were five sounds. I asked, "where do you go for inspiration in yourself?" and she said, "Prospect Park. The light shining down through the trees." So we did this piece, from one side of the room to the other. It was so quiet. And at the end of it we were both just weeping -- because it was beautiful. And it was just the two of us. And it wasn't therapy. We weren't trying to get anywhere. I wasn't trying to make anything happen. It was just simply setting up a world where something that wanted to come forward, could. And we could feel it.

We all know when we're with somebody who's willing to be present with us. We all know it. We all know it when we are being talked down to. We all know it when we are being taken somewhere, you know, and to come into a space as an artist, as a community source artist and hold that center of gravity and say, this is going to be a place of beauty, or investigation, and I don't mean beauty as in something that's pretty, or sounds nice. I'm not talking about that. I'm talking about beauty as something that feels truthful. I don't know. I have no definition about beauty but it just feels like mm! you know? This is real!

So that started me on the journey, and I went to bigger and bigger projects. And the context I want to give to you is that in... 2005? I got a call from Ireland, "Would you come do a project for the European Festival of Culture? We want you to do inter-generational work." I had already started to do inter-generational work. Why? Because it feels good. It feels right. This is very recent that some of us, born into cultures of adolescents, are like, "Ooh, Lets put our elders in a building and freak out when we go in there". You know, it's recent. So, inter-generational work -- Yeah! great! I went over there and I chose a spot in a nursing home for homeless adults and an Alzheimer's unit. I'm just going to tell the story because I love talking about failure. There's a lot of things I love talking about in this work, and one is failure. The other one is the truth of partnerships and collaboration, like -- get real! The other one is the shadow of the word, "community." The other one is animating spaces. The other one is ethics and integrity. The other one is -- where is the art? You know, I mean, seriously like these are all things I love to talk about, and wish we could all talk about forever, because that would mean I love you. I'll make you mediocre food -- I promise you. [laughter]

So anyway, you know, I go there and do this project and we have Irish artists, and a few of us from the States, and we have community members, and we make the last supper. You can see it online. It's under the Littleglobe video link. Go watch it. It's beautiful. Six months long we sit around the big table, we do experimental video. We make a Gamelan out of tea cups. Beautiful, what the heck! People stop using eye patches. They stop using canes. They feel like they belong. Belonging -- our primary impulse for survival of human beings. The thing that's most important to us, even if we think it's not. Apparently. Okay, they start to feel like they belong, and I'm freaked out as an artist. It never occurred to me that a project is going to actually change someone's life, and what is my responsibility towards that. This is one of your questions. What's our responsibility?

Okay, we create a beautiful piece. We have the performances at the site, they're sold out. The staff goes through a freak out experience where they're like, "the participants can't do that!" I was like, "Let's include all the staff" and they were like, "No!" The staff was very caught between power structures and sense of identity, and it was tough. At the end they just sat in the audience, crying, because they had no idea that the people they lived with everyday, had that in them.

And the piece happens, it's beautiful! How much money did I leave for the artists to continue work in Ireland? $6000. I took no time to build ongoing partnerships. I got three emails, two months later. Michael, Anne, and one other person have all fallen into depression. That's unethical. But it never occurred to me, as artists, that we have that power. Not that we have power, but that we might be doing something powerful. Like really!

So it changed my life, and I'm going to speak to you today as somebody, who -- Look, I have the artistic impulse to, you know, do all sorts of things that don't have years and years of commitment. But both projects that I am going to talk about -- Lifesongs is a project that became a program. Those are two very different things. And COAL, to which I've made a ten year commitment, and I'm on year three, and if I look scraped and bruised, I am. I speak to you today, and I'm leaving at 11pm tonight to New York City, to a full COAL development workshop with Broadway musical actors. We're out of money. The Climate March just listed COAL on their website. We are not ready to disseminate. I mean, I can tell you crazy things, and why would you ever choose a topic as impersonal as climate, like why not just grow beets and do a project on local beets. It's really a better idea. But I'm going to tell you why I thought it was a good idea.

So I'm going to start with a story from Mary. Mary Gilmore. You are looking at Mary Gilmore [on slide]. Mary Gilmore, I met the first year we started Lifesongs. The Santa Fe Opera had commissioned me to do a community opera. I'm not going to talk about that project, but I started a relationship with Santa Fe Care Center. I walked in there and I was like -- What the heck is this place? Has anybody been there? Okay. 85%

of the people there don't have active visitors. If you haven't gone, go, because it's good to go. Santa Fe Care Center. It's a nursing home. I met Mary, and Mary had advanced dementia. I didn't have any idea what I was doing. Christine introduces me to her and I was like, "Hey, what if we tried writing music with people who don't really come out of their rooms much?" Mary was kind of amazing. She had all these Guadalupe bracelets on, and she always wore matching velour suits which I thought was fantastic. They were green or purple. She was very feisty, and the distinguishing quality about Mary is that I took a mini keyboard in, and I was like, "Hey Mary, what kind of sound do you like?" and we played through these sounds, and she loved really dissonant, dense chords. That is not common. People often really want to hear something that resolves and sounds familiar to them. Oh my god, she was anything but that. Mary was pissed off. Angry, angry, angry, and one of the things about doing the kind of relationally based public art that I do, is that I'm really interested in anything that's alive with somebody, or in a community. So if that's heavy metal, if that is like, "I'm so pissed at you, and your eyebrow makes me super irritated" I'm interested in the eyebrow! I think we're probably all like that. You follow what's alive, right? I think one of the things about being an artist in this kind of work, is having the facility to know when to step back and lift up their voice, and to know when to step in with artistic will and direction, and say, "Let's try this direction, and it may not work, but let's try that." So that kind of muscle is something that I feel is developed over time; I think it's a continuum. The continuum of moving, and it can happen within a ten minute frame. You know what I'm saying? So Mary -- Oh Mary was pissed, pissed, pissed, and she did not know why she was in a nursing home. Okay?

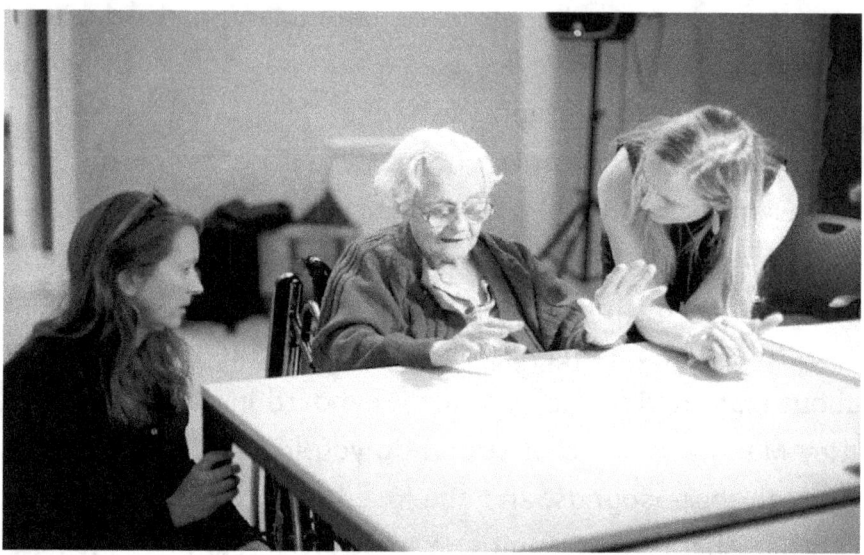

Lifesongs

So I'm going to sing you a little bit of Mary's song. It took about 3 months and we wrote it. The end of this song is: "What am I going to do for Christmas? I don't know. Just sit here, just sit here all day long and try to be helpful."

We sing this song at every Lifesongs concert. Why? because the main theme I'm going to talk about with both these projects, is Shadow. And if we don't get some air into that shadow land, collectively, around death and dying, we lose our ability to really live vitally, and in a good way. I see it again and again. The grief cycle, and death and dying, aging. If we don't come to terms with it, individually and collectively, we are lost. I really believe that, the more I'm on this project. The first year we did Mary's song, we were like, "Huh, what would it be like if young people sang the songs that people write at the end of their lives?" The Santa Fe Choir showed up. It was the worst prepping we had ever done. They showed up and you can see how they were dressed, while the elders were really dignified. This never happened again, but that was kind of funny.

Christine Sandoval, here, is one of my longest term partners -- seven years. And everything I'm going to talk about here has to do with partnership relationships, because, to do projects that animate spaces that aren't already animated, usually there's some really deep partnerships going on. And those are not to be taken lightly or messed with or tokenized. They are real. To do long term real projects, there has to be some chemistry and some real understanding, and some ways to get through breakdowns. Because otherwise, it's just a mess, and I know we all know it. So I take the partnerships I'm in very seriously, and they tend to be very long term now. It doesn't end up just being professional. We're creating our communities, we're creating our lives, we're creating our hearts. If we're going to do community sourced work, and relational work, I think it's something to really look at. How we think about partnerships. Because people say that word all the time, and I'm like, "What the heck do you mean?" Like really? And if we're not transparent about it, what do you want from a partnership? That's a mess. That's a mess -- usually everybody has needs, individual needs, ambitious. It's good to be honest about it. We're all the same, you know, different variations. Christine Sandoval-- amazing! Lifesongs wouldn't have happened without her.

Mary's song was last performed at the Lensic by Brooke,

and there's Mary. This is the first year of Lifesongs. Mary, Barbara Armstrong, and Juanita Durham. It was our first three Lifesongs. Barbara died the day after her Lifesong was performed. She stood up there with her flowers and said, "I can't believe I did this!" She wrote a piece called 'The Dark Sea' -- "I am searching for life, I am searching for life in the dark sea." Mary Gilmore died 3 days later. They both stood up, happy as can be, that day. Juanita is still alive. Okay. Forgive me.

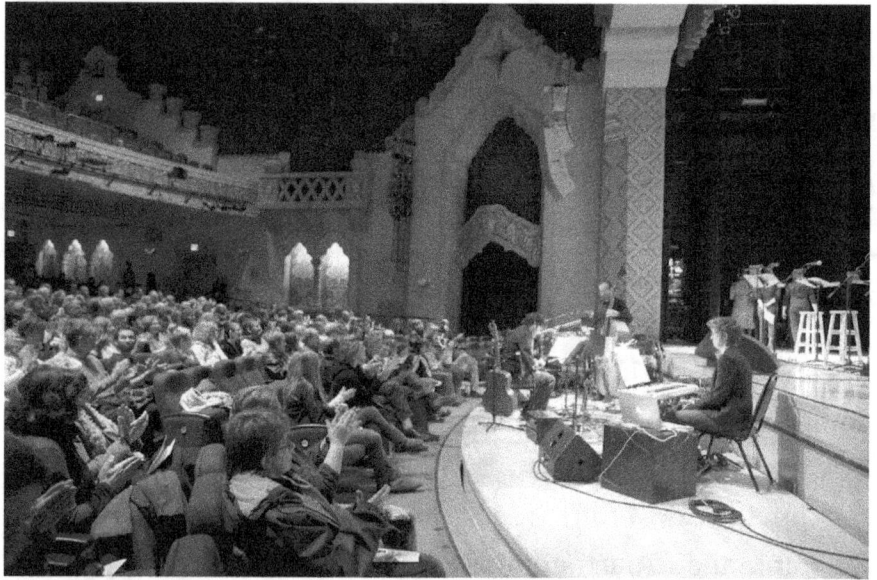

Lifesongs

(Molly Sturges singing song)

What caused the fall? I can't remember.

Help me get out of here. Help me get out of here.

Lord...Lord, I'm talking to you, Lord -- Oh please, my Lord, hear me.

What I want is what I had before, what I want is what I had before.

What caused the fall?

I can't remember.

Help me get out of here. Help me get out of here.

Lord... What will I do at Christmas?

I will sit here. I will sit here all day long and try to be helpful.

[applause]

Mary Gilmore... pretty rich, pretty deep. We can all feel it, and one thing about the Lifesongs project, I believe, is that it has a heart that most of us can feel.

I'm just going to show you some images and then I'm going to show you a little video. This is Barbara and her family. One thing we didn't realize, going into this project. We write music with people in hospice and community groups. We have a Lifesongs choir right now. Hopefully soon the Lifesongs village band that sings the songs of the elders. We have a new site going up. There's a lot of different elements. The program is growing, but we're probably not going to grow that large. We're keeping our focus a lot on the research and pedagogy, so you've got a group of artists that are really trying to figure out, "How do we do this? What's happening actually when we do this work?" It's almost research. What's actually happening? There's a lot going on, and a lot of what Aly talked about, resonated with the issue of relational listening in this work. And I talk about presence, but I don't think really any of us know exactly what constitutes presence. But I think there's something about being an artist where you come into a space, and facilitate this kind of connecting and artistic inquiry, and the space opens up, partially by the amount of work you've done in yourself. I know that if I haven't done my own work on death and dying -- which I swear to god, I have not done all of it -- but more and more, it opens up new spaces. Then there's a million other factors, like who's there, and the partnership, and how it's been. There's so many factors in how this work gets done, and what it really means or what you want as an artist. I'm such a fan of the rogue artist. I just want to say, that's my heart, but my life has just led me in a different direction, you know, and now this is what it is.

So, families are a great part of Lifesongs, and this is Francisco Romero and myself, we were working with a compositional tool of composing by moving your hands. I'll show you that in the video. This is often what a session looks like. Spending a lot of time listening, being with somebody in hospice as they discover something that means something to them that they want to share. Just having the space. Meeting somebody where they are, putting unlikely collaborators together. This is a young girl from the Santa Fe Opera Voices singing with Michael Tafoya, who has advanced Parkinson's, and they did a duet together. Looks like this. You know, you see this and you're like, "Oh, it's social work." It's not, you know, it's not. We are all artists in this room. What's a real artist? I know when I meet people who are really rigorous in their investigations. It's awesome, but I tell you the minute you get involved with institutions, stuff gets flattened. The language changes. Why? Because you have to change the language for people to understand it or relate to it. It's a pain, but it happens. How do we keep the artistic work vital? It's hard, it's a tightrope. Sometimes the vital art is there and sometimes it's not. There are so many community arts projects with hands in them, and I love Chrissie's work to death, and she knows it, but I'm just like, "really, enough of the hands" -- but you know that's not too Chrissie. It's just too all of us, but we're all trying to find participatory frames, right? Participatory frames, how we animate spaces, that's a lot of what we do. That's why this collective knowledge is so important, because we're all learning tons, and we have been for a long time, but a lot of things work better than other things, and we all fail, and we have to be learning together.

Aurelia Gomez... one of the things about these elders, is that we're losing huge amounts of earth-based knowledge. Okay, Aurelia knows a lot about growing chiles and it's not just a trite thing. She actually knows a lot. So we're losing huge amounts of information right now, and you guys know this, but it's just a big deal.

The UNM choir is another partnership.

This is what the Lensic concerts look like. We found that we lost a lot of intimacy at the Lensic... and, they're a great partner.

This is a community of nurses, a choir that sings to people when they're dying. The Threshold Choir -- did you know that they exist? They come to people's beds. [Molly sings] "We love you...." beautiful! These nurses come over, and they sing to you, when you're dying or sick. I want them to sing to me every morning.

This was this year's, and you can see that there's about as many participants as there are audience. That's how I like it. We don't want passive audiences. I'm not interested in that, not really interested in passivity.

Okay, I'm going to show you a little video, and then I'm going to move onto COAL.

If you have questions write them down.

See video at www.evolvingintentionsinpublicart.org

So what are some of the things you noticed or felt watching that? Anybody out there want to tell me?

Audience Member:

Lack of Kleenex boxes right now!

Audience Member:

I was really moved by your work, and everything I've seen here, and what I want to share with you is that -- I came from a very lost village in Africa, and I've been in the West for less than 20 years, and everything I hear is beauty and heart. I don't think when you say beauty and heart, it means what you see or what you hear. I think it's the transformation we have in the human soul. That's beauty and heart. I teach art, and I think all forms of art are public, because we start thinking in our studio, in our room, or bathroom, then we take it outside, and people have to react to it. They may be inspired, be moved, and I think that's beauty in the heart, so thank you.

Molly Sturges:

Thank you. One more, then we'll move onto COAL.

Audience Member:

It actually follows from Aly's presentation too, if you could say something more on the role of witnessing. And maybe because you come from an activist background as well, and your experience of witnessing in Lifesongs -- what it gives to you. What arises in you about the role of witnessing and activism?

Molly Sturges:

I know you've done more thinking about this than I have my dear.

I was just teaching up in Alaska with a novelist named Luis Urrea, who wrote *The Hummingbird's Daughter*. A really great author and activist. He's from Tijuana. He talks about being an "author of witness" as his work. He brings this vital creativity and storytelling to working with people in these giant dump communities, trash communities, in Tijuana, and also to border guards and border crossings. I'm just thinking of him being asked this question, because he and I had a lot of time to talk about this.

Witnessing, it's a really interesting thing for me, because I don't know that it's actually enough for me anymore, as a concept. I think it's something I would have wrapped myself around a lot more in the past. I think about that Lilla Watson quote, "If you've come to help me you're wasting your time. But if you have come because your liberation is bound up with mine, then let us work together."

That rings really, really true for me. When I work, I refer a lot to a study I read on global wellbeing. I'm not talking about the happiness study. Three primary impulses for wellbeing globally:

1. Good relationships

2. Feeling connected to something larger than ourselves

3. Meaningful participation

You look at El Otro Lado. A lot of people around these days do not feel like they have a way to meaningfully participate. You go to the nursing home, nobody's listening -- is anybody witnessing what's going on there? Yeah, the staff is. The people go in there and there's this wealth of knowledge. Hospice workers, for god's sake, they know so much. How is that information being shared, circulated, pollinated, on a societal level, to increase our capacity to be better, more loving, caring, just and sustainable communities? How is that happening? I think a lot of that's happening by people in this room. I think we are plumbers, a lot of us. We are plumbing. We're hooking up all sorts of things. It's exhausting, It's difficult. We witness a lot. It's hard to hold! It's hard to support each other. It's hard to survive it. It's hard to get through depression. It's hard to deal with the funding situation. It's hard work. It's leadership work. It's some of the most important leadership work I think that's going on.

Back to witnessing. One thing I notice about relationships. Not so much connected to "something larger" -- I think that's where the art work comes in, the deep art part of this is helping us feel connected to something larger. The thing about good relationships and meaningful participation, both, to me, have to do with artists and people like us, cultural workers, who are able to go into situations -- and we are, and we are feeling things and taking things in on multiple levels. All of us, multiple levels. We are seeing the status quo that doesn't work, we're seeing a vision of something that's possible, we're creating situations were people can express themselves. If there's no expression, there's no connection, if there's no connection there's no democracy. That's how I see it. If somebody can't express how pissed off they are, or happy or sad or despondent, or they want to commit suicide, how are you going to feel connection? You can't. So artists, to me, are doing this invaluable thing. I hear my voice, and somebody's listening to me, somebody sees me, somebody is witnessing this situation. Does that make sense as an answer so far? I don't have an answer for you, and I'd like to talk about it with you. I don't have an answer, I just have all these sort of mushy ideas.

I want to move onto COAL is that okay?

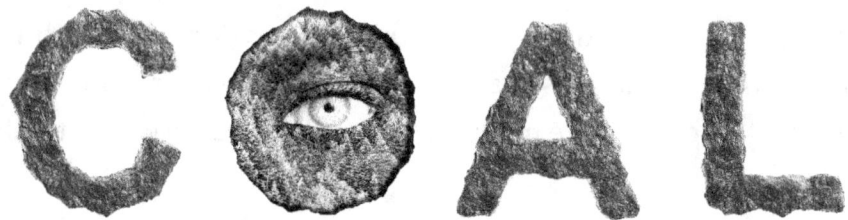

Who in their right mind takes on something like COAL? [laughter] Why would you do it? Okay, it's just a bad idea as an artist, right? I want to tell you why it happened. Some years ago I had this opportunity, and some money and time, and I was like, "What am I not addressing as an artist?" I thought to myself, surely it's climate change. You know, like, I have a kid. So I started researching everything and at that time -- it's changing a lot right now -- but at that time, there were a lot of documentary projects, really good ones, like-- look how bad it's going to be. Like scare projects, right? But one thing we know is that, yes, that's helpful -- *Chasing Ice* is helpful -- but what's helpful about it is the personal story, as well, that we can connect to. Climate is this giant topic. I've started my talk a number of times with, "What's the difference between a climate and a vagina?" Because I think COAL is like the Vagina Monologues project, but different. What's the difference? Well, we can all say we've had a very intimate relationship with a vagina. We came through it or we're interested in them or we have them or hopefully we all love them. But, climate is like-- What? as a concept-- does anybody know? Climate--I don't even know what it is. It's so abstract. and so when I came across this book-- *Coal- A Human History*, in the book it said "Coal is the story of creation, destruction. It's the interplay between those two that is so compelling." I was like-- that's mythical! We are dealing on a mythical level, people, and so I just came up with this idea of: I'm going to make a mythical musical fable. It's going to be scalable. Communities can use it, churches, theaters. We can do it around our dinner table. It's going to be a big musical. Geez, I guess I'll start with the songs.

That was a really bad idea. Slowed me down by a year. I'm sure at least some of you have seen the COAL trailer. Okay, I'm just going to play it again. It's a little outdated, but currently was just listed on the Climate March site, I think I told you that. It's kind of outdated but you can hear some of the music, and get some of the approach to it. Then I'm going to just talk a little bit about what it's really like to do this project, and bring up some issues that maybe we can touch on later.

See video at www.evolvingintentionsinpublicart.org

Thank you. There's a concept trailer for you, and how the project has changed! No, it really hasn't changed that much actually. It's kind of weird actually how far we've gone, and how much we've come back. COAL -- okay, I want to talk about scaling intimacy. A lot of us are involved in very local projects. I love local projects. I wanted to create a catalytic template. It's not new. Bill T. Jones has done it. A lot of artists have done it. There's a climate ribbon tree being done right now. There's all sorts of templates that communities can take and make their own. You have to simplify stuff a lot. You can hear the music. The music was designed to be very accessible, to defy what you might think of as a musical about climate change. It's not really folk music. You hear the banjo a few times, but it's not Appalachian music.

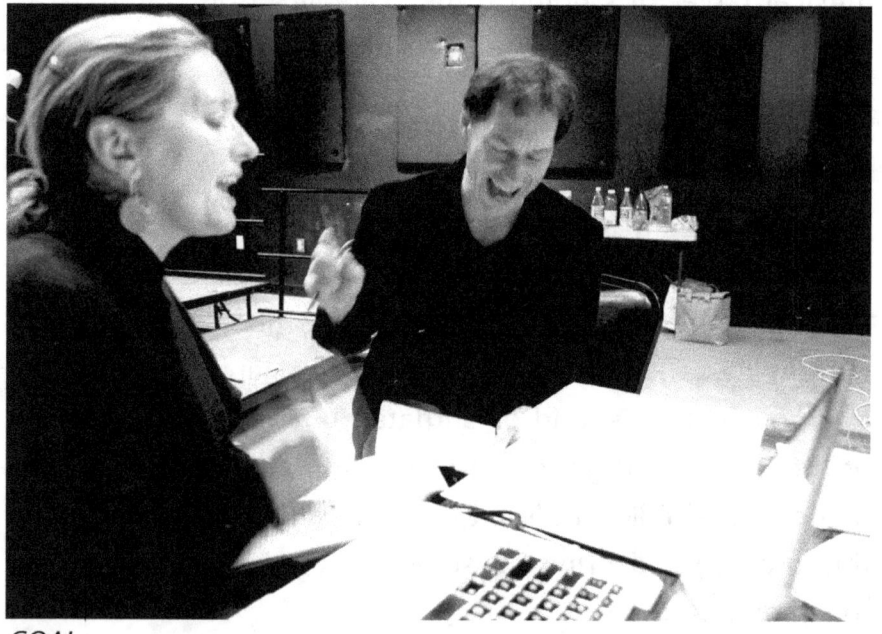

COAL

I was talking with a guy in Kentucky and he said, "Coal really isn't an issue in my community; they're doing mountain top mining up there about 100 miles away." and I was like, "Wow! Coal burned anywhere is coal burned everywhere." Do you know how much of our electricity comes from coal in New Mexico? 60%. The rest of it is nuclear and mostly natural gas. Right now I'm on a steering committee for developing a municipal energy grid, where we can make our own energy choices, and my biggest dream is that all of us artists would engage that fully. That is my dream. And you can talk to me about that if you'd like to. But it's a very concrete thing, it's a very real thing. Coal is the number one culprit in global warming. It is burning the future so quickly, it's amazing.

It's really hard to get. I'm not saying this for any guilt, you know -- we can all feel it in our body, what happens when we start thinking about these big things. It kind of hurts. Do you feel like you shut down a little bit? I always do. I feel smaller, and kind of tighter... and you know, you have to kind of choose a way from that. You have to breathe a little bigger, actually, because overwhelm is not a stopping point. But we are not alone. None of us is alone.

So starting a project like this, one of the things I did was talk to a lot of climate behaviorologists. It's a whole industry, it turns out. People are overwhelmed. You get overwhelmed very quickly. It's too big, and people come out of experiences and they say, "One: I didn't know, and two: I don't know what to do." So you need a sense of connection, and you also have to feel like you're part of the solution, it turns out. There have to be metaphors. Right now we're seeing the largest climate march ever, in New York City. Bobbe already talked about the events here. What's happening is there's a shift in identity happening, all over. It's been going on for awhile, but it's happening more and more and more. So the thing is, to watch ourselves when we feel guilty or overwhelmed, and as an artist, I feel like I need to address that in the project. So I address it in the story. I address it in the songs. Not in a overt way, but multiple opportunities for us to feel personal connection to something first of all, then to have a space to express oneself, and then to have a sense of what can be done practically in your own community. So that involves partnerships, right?

I committed ten years to this project, I think I told you that. That's kind of a big commitment, and it's been really hard. It's really hard to face this stuff on a regular basis and not turn away from it, and it's hard to hold it as the artistic director, to say, "No you guys, we're going to keep on going -- It may not be the right thing but hopefully it will be something that will contribute." And you just try, right? We're all doing that. We're all just trying.

I think I'm weepy right now because I'm about to go to New York and have two weeks to actually just work on the music, and I am above all a musician, and I haven't had the opportunity to do that. To go to the heart of each song and say: "What lives here?" It's a relief. All that other music was fricking written at 2am in the morning. I'd sit up in my bed, and be like, "There was a sleep and ooze a snooze that made them forget..."You know, it's like 2am in the morning. Really bad recordings, and I'd send it to Luis in L.A. and he'd send some stuff back. It wasn't that satisfying. We just slapped it up there. So, nobody's alone, there's no right answer. This is a situation of total disorientation.

Right now so many of our indigenous leaders up in Canada are working so hard in communities against the Tar Sands. I was just teaching with Winona LaDuke. We have hunger strikes going on. Hunger strikes! I think if I didn't have a kid, I'd be doing a hunger strike, probably. I'm just giving you very personal words for how it is to work on a project like this, and part of it is just that the topic is too big. It's overwhelming. Everybody's doing local work and bringing it down to scale -- It just means so much to me, because it helps me ground here.

The other thing I want to say about COAL, and then I'll open up to questions, is what it means to do an open-sourced template. I've done tests with a church in Orange County, and what they told me is that they wanted to have their youth in the piece, so we wrote choral arrangements for it, and they tried that out. I went to the University of North Carolina and did a two-person version, and they were like, "We've done all the community engagement stuff." We got there and I was

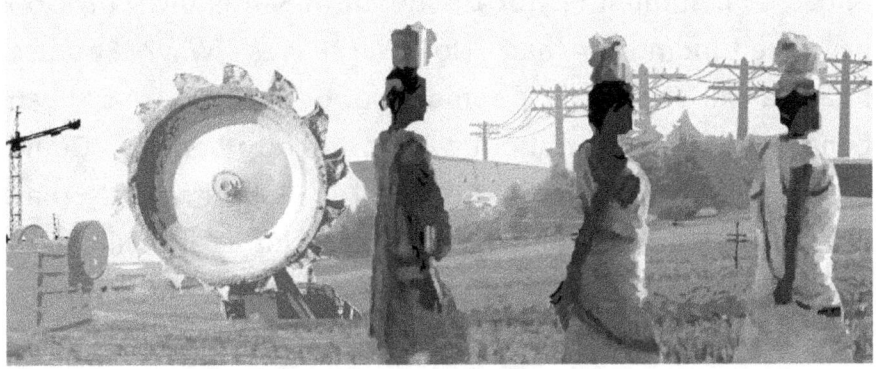

COAL

like, "Where, where?" "We're having wine together." "That's not community engagement!" "What, have the Sierra Club here?" I was like-- Oh my God, we have to put videos on our site. Here's the things to think about. Here's what we think about when we talk about how to engage. Here's how to do a dialogue where actually, it's not the question -- and please don't ever say this to me -- "Who's at the table?" Well is it your table? I mean, I just can't take it. I think we really have to rethink how we are collaborating deeply with people. Really! So to make an inclusive circle, you're going to ask people to come forward and feel safe to really contribute? That's an art. There are a lot of practices, and it turns out they're thousands of years old, that are doing this work. We have this knowledge among us. We could sit down together and get it really right, you know.

So, that was a big wakeup call. I'm now in collaboration with a high school in North Carolina that's going to be training their own performance team, at the high school, to then go out to elementary schools and do it. In 2015 we'll be at three stops along the Montana coal train route, developing it with directly impacted communities for the debut in San Francisco. Do I have the funding for that? No. Will I? Yes. Why? Because I have a will of steel. Or something, or a willow tree. I can bend. I am very clear about what's going to happen. Could the timeline be delayed? Yes. Will it look differently than what I imagined? Absolutely. Will I cry a lot? Yes. Will I have unexpected sources of joy? Yes. You know, that's how it's going to be. Will it be successful? I have no idea you guys, I have no idea. It seems to be working, the signs are there. So that's my truth telling about COAL. Is that helpful at all or interesting? I don't even know.

One thing I want to say, just artistically. When we do open it up, open-source, after the big debut -- I just want to say, I didn't want to do the big musical. I wanted to go straight

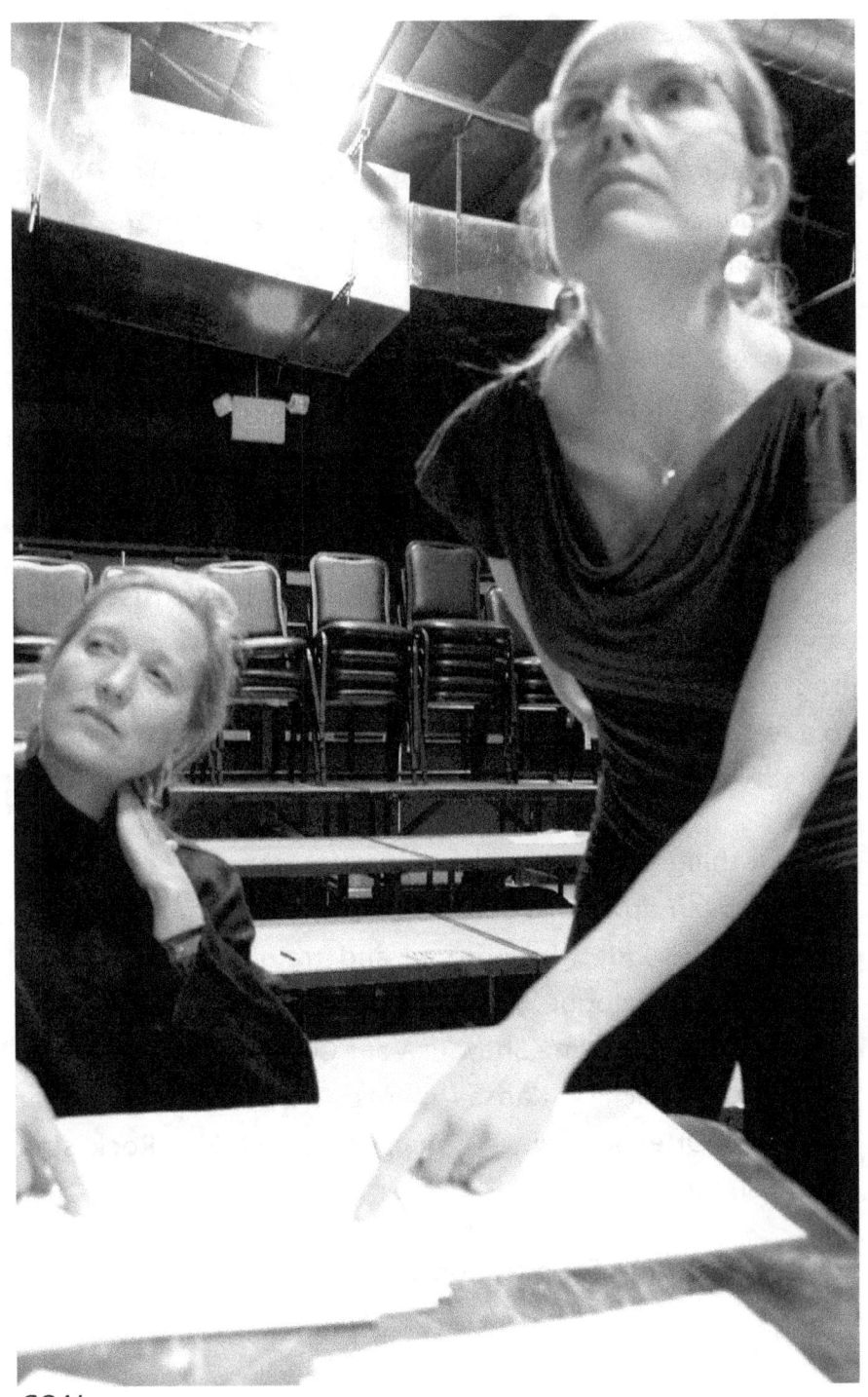

COAL

grassroots, because that's where my heart is. I'm mad about going. I'm happy to go to New York and engage with with a whole industry of musical theater, but I'm also like-- ehnh... alright. But the reason I'm doing this, is because I brought in a producer and a director who know a lot more about scale than I do. Everybody's volunteering. Everybody's grumpy, exhausted. Seriously, we work so hard and we are exhausted. However, they know about scale and I don't. As a founder, I keep drawing things back to the original feeling I had. And that's not right for the project. As an artistic director I have to keep the vision and the heart there, but as a founder I have to let it go past my level of discomfort. Am I worried? Yes. Does it feel weird? Yes, but I trust them, I think. I try to trust them. That's just an example of a program growing and changing, and knowing what you can do as a founder/artist, and maybe what you can't do, when it starts to scale bigger.

The last thing is, when people can open-source -- check this out -- you can download scores for guitar, piano, choir. You can download video backdrops, and training videos about how to do the dialogue. It's all there for people, and then we say, "Make it your own. Show us your COAL now." What does it look like in Wichita, Kansas? What does it look like? What does your Otter look like? What does your Fire Rock sing like? You know.

So let's open it up for questions.

Audience Member:

First of all, thank you so much for being here, and thank you so much for the work that you do. I was wondering if you could talk a little more about what you do when you work with groups of people in the community. What it is that you actually do?

Molly Sturges:

That's a really good question. It depends on the project. I've done a lot of different kinds of projects with community groups -- all this stuff is going to be really familiar to you guys -- but I always do a lot of talking with people ahead of time, a lot. A lot of open listening with people. We're starting in Kingston -- I'll go spend the whole week, before I start there, just going to sessions, listening to people. We all do this as artists, and I think, very unexpected things are going to happen during that time period. So, being very open to the unexpected. Somebody will come forward and say something that just shifts the whole project. Or there's a relationship made that grounds it in a whole different way. I really see that as part of the project. I do not isolate out an artistic product from the relationship building. I think that is a really important part of this creative practice for me is; it's one whole thing -- including the follow-up. What we call follow-up. That is not an after project thing. That's THE project. The next thing, is that I really look at obstacles of participation. Sometimes people will say -- "Oh look, nobody came to the survey that we did at the Lensic at 11am on Tuesday." I wonder why. Why do you think? people work, you know. So, food, childcare,Pthat costs money. So that might mean I have to start my project ahead of time. Gathering those basic resources and figuring a lot of time into research and development and relationship building. Usually people can understand that and will respect it because it will show the depth of your thinking and respect for the community, and the project, and their time. So, we've been in Diné communities where people were like, "Nobody's going to participate." and we had 150 people come on a Saturday. Why? Because we spent four months talking with people. We had food, childcare. Guess what? The women, the mothers, the very people they said wouldn't come, all came and wanted to stay late, each time. Why? Because it was an open space where we're not told who you had to be. Why? Because your kids could be safe and comfortable there. Why? Because you had a few hours to not have to do some other big thing. Why? Because it's unexpected. It's art, it's about discovery. We are in the best business in the world. Imagination and discovery, what could be better? But the amount of work to set that up is really huge.

So gathering, and then we create stuff. We always create stuff, and then we have a chance to share it. We saw that in El Otro Lado. When somebody stands up, and says their thing -- I don't care who they are, how they did it -- you stand up and say your thing, it will change the molecules in your body, if you've not been heard before like that. When the whole Cuba, New Mexico group came to the Lensic to perform, after our project there, 350 people witnessed a group of kids, elders, community members from Torreon, Ojo Encino -- very remote eastern Navajo communities -- each one of them said to me at the end, "That meant something, to be received." I had thought-- The Lensic's the wrong place, we should do the Rodeo Grounds. Then I realized, no, no, the Lensic is a place of power, and to stand on that stage and have a group of artists with them saying, "This is beautiful, and you are powerful." They stood on that stage... I had no idea -- I wasn't prepared for it, what it would mean to people in their lives.

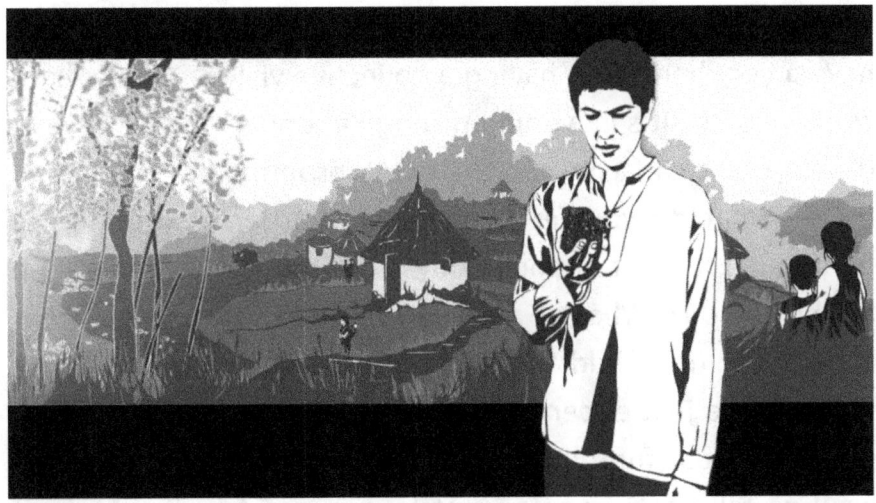

COAL

We share. We do a lot of ongoing evaluation. "How is that for you? What's going on?" Constant reciprocal learning going on, and then always an eye to capacity building. Am I leading something, or is somebody else with me leading it too? So that that community has ownership over its own capacity, if I'm not going to be there. Does that make sense? There's more to it than that, but... in the circle itself, anything can happen, but there's an awful lot of balance between framing things. I think a lot of it comes from how we are be-ing.

Audience Member:

Do you direct the conversation to be specifically about climate change?

Molly Sturges:

With COAL? Oh my god, COAL rests increasingly on the songs, and the questions that are asked in the songs. "What is a good life? What is a war? What is your war?" We know what we are against, but we often do not know what we are for. We have a very hard time having a collective vision. That's hard work, people. It's like going through a tunnel, and we have to develop that capacity. So the COAL prompts are everything from, "What do you feel?... What do you want your life to be about?... What is somebody from the future generation saying to you? What do they say to you right now?... What do you say to a child three generations from now?" I don't know, we're just experimenting. We just ask people to help us. We're just fumbling here. But to have space -- people want to talk, and people want to grieve. And if you don't have a grieving cycle, you don't have possibility. You have trauma. We are all grieving. Even if you think you're blocking that stuff out and you don't believe in it, I swear to you, you're grieving. We're constantly evolving that.

We're working on a visual arts activity that any community can do. It's based on Peruvian drawings with natural materials, that you do in small groups. So you're creating something beautiful, but each material is a different prompt. We're looking at different ideas. We eat together. We always eat together. If I'm not eating with somebody I get nervous. [laughter]

Audience Member:

These lights are on today because of coal. That's where our power comes from in New Mexico, and remember that, when you turn your lights on. If you wish to do a little something, a small piece, the People's Climate March in Santa Fe is taking place here on September 20th. Bring your art, bring your costume, bring your drum, bring something. We're meeting at the plaza at noon, and there will be a march that goes to the Railyard and -- just show up. We really need your art, your ideas, your enthusiasm and your presence.

In deep gratitude for Molly's work in community and engagement. That's a critical part of everything. Thank you.

Molly Sturges:

Thank you. I did an article a few years ago with some organizers from SWOP - Southwest Organizing Project. We worked with them and it's called Direct and Indirect Approaches to Social Change, and I just want to say why I did that -- I just want to be very honest. Rallies, I go to them, but I have a really hard time with them. Why? I don't know. I feel like the culture has to be updated, and remade. I was at a climate march recently and the chanting was horrible. I was like-- I can't do it, I can't do this chant. I mean, everybody needs to go, but what I'm trying to say is, "Artists, let's remake this shit." We're Santa Fe! You know, and I promise to convene in a space like that, but let's remake it so we feel something when we do it. It's going to be a beautiful rally, but I want to just say, this is ours to do. Right? This is ours to do. Bring our artistry and make it beautiful -- I think we can open spaces as artists. We can invigorate, and the format is struggling to update right now. We are struggling to have songs. Songs were the central thing of the apartheid movement. What are we singing? "No more war." We're not singing, people! This is a big problem, and I don't want to just sit around and say later, "Well, I never addressed the problem." Let's address the problem, people!

It's very hard for artists to deal with political short term goals sometimes. Political practices have a lot of short term goals that we need to reach, and so artists end up being transactional. Like: Here's a banner you can use, or here's a logo you can use. Well most of us are not doing art because of that reason. It's different than that. So I think it's an uneasy marriage that I'm involved in, and maybe some of you are involved in, and that's okay. Let it be messy, and let it be uneasy.

Just to end with this, when I started COAL, somebody said: "You have to choose between being an artist and an activist on this project. You're going to have to choose." So, I'm just saying to you, honestly, I do experience that as a paradox sometimes. In terms of the open-ended space, and the goal space. The fact that we actually need wins for community organizing. You have to feel like you're actually doing something. But it's okay for me that the paradox exists. I don't believe it's a choice. I said to him: "I think that's a really outdated way of looking at this." There's an undulating space, an undefined undulating space that has all of it, and that's where I live, if I can.

Thank you very much, and thanks, Christy, for having me.

[Applause]

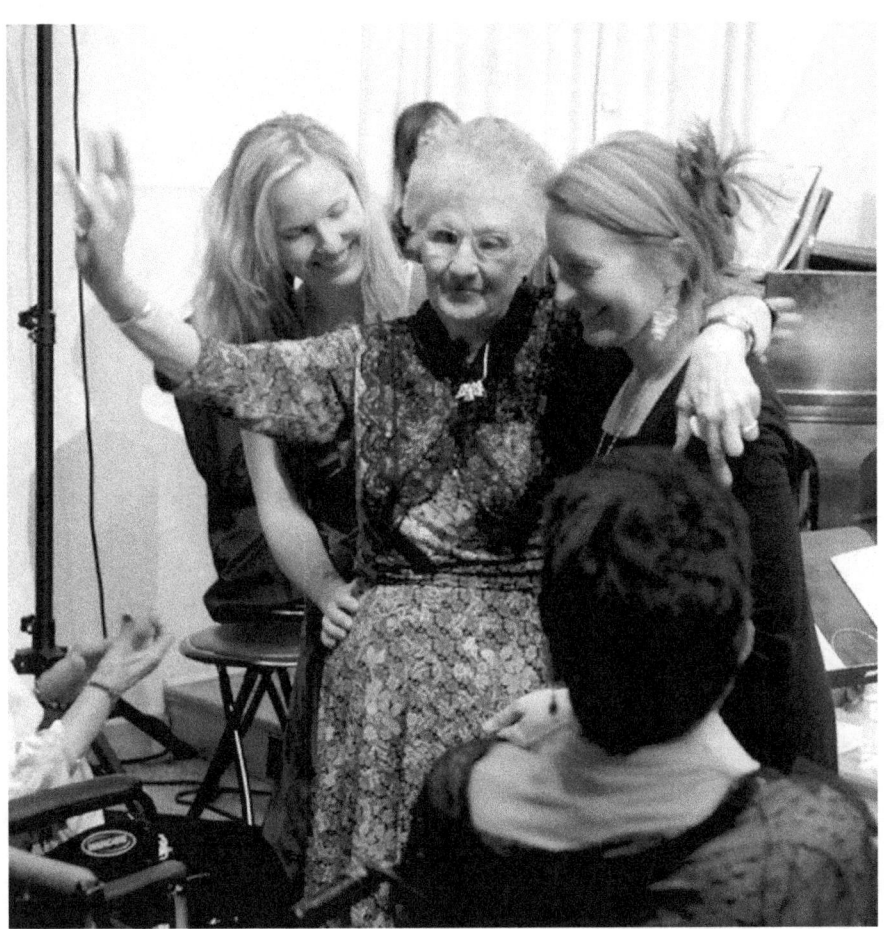

Lifesongs

Edie Tsong

CUT + PASTE SOCIETY

SNOW POEMS

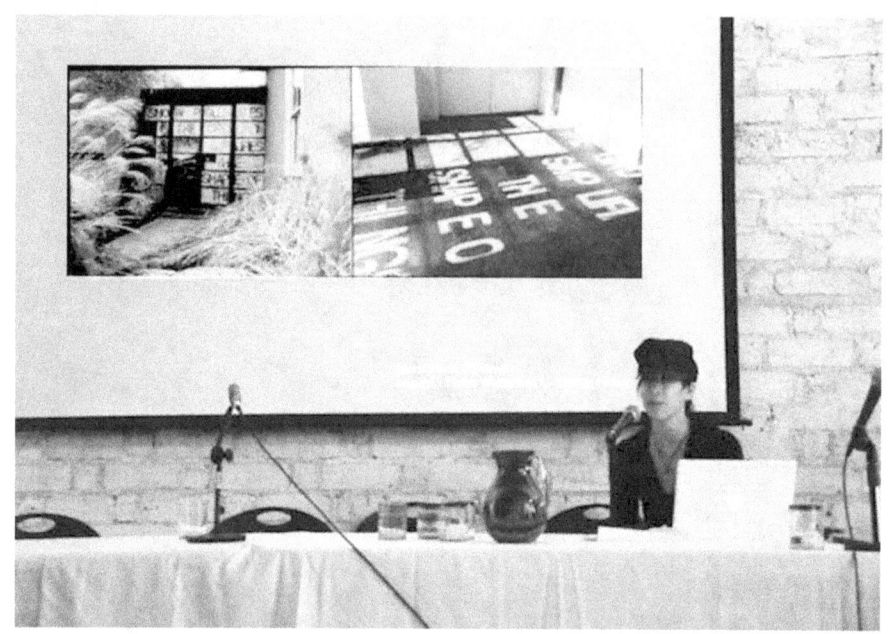

Edie Tsong

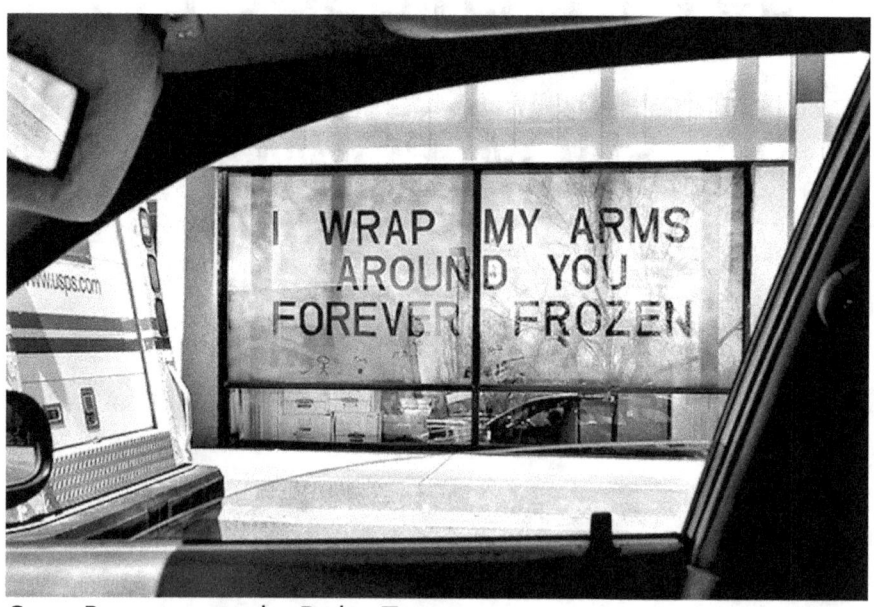

Snow Poems, poem by Pedro Tena

Edie Tsong:

Hi everyone. If I had known I was going to be this nervous I would have brought a big stuffed animal to sit with me up here. [laughter] I know you guys are all friends and there are so many mentors here, collaborators here, but for whatever reason, I still feel panicked. Anyway, let's get into this.

My name is Edie Tsong, and I'm the founder of Cut + Paste Society, and I'm going to be giving a talk called the Autobiography of the Snow Poems Project. If you were here in Santa Fe two years ago, or even three years ago, you may have seen the poems around the city that were stenciled on windows. There were poems on sixty windows of forty different buildings around the city. They included three elementary schools, a middle school, a high school, Santa Fe Community College, Santa Fe University of Art and Design, and county, city and state buildings, two public libraries, and a lot of independent businesses. That was the visible part of the project, but it's kind of like an iceberg where, that was just what was visible, and there was so much so much underneath that.

I tortured myself over what I would say, and now I feel totally different. I don't even know what I want to say, but I really want to begin with the starting point of me as an artist. I grew up in Pennsylvania, with Taiwanese parents, and everything that we have heard this morning about the sense of belonging and needing to be witnessed, those are all things that I grew up without, and have really shaped the way I have been an artist. Snow Poems, for me, when we wash them away -- I was the one who was in the middle of organizing this project -- even though we worked with Cut + Paste Society and the Santa Fe Art Institute, everything led back to me -- and when the poems were washed away, I remember this distinct feeling of standing at the Santa Fe Community Gallery and looking down Grant Avenue, and seeing the empty window on the Teen Court where there had been a poem, and just having this feeling like: Were the poems just an excuse so we could talk to each other? Were they an excuse so we could connect with each other? So we could be connected to the place where we live, together? That's been a theme running through all of my work, having grown up in central Pennsylvania. If you can imagine a little Asian girl in Penn State football culture, trying to fit in. So that's what it's about.

My gateway drug into the arts was through ceramics. I did not want to be an artist, because I couldn't understand the reason why it was important. What I did know was that, after going through high school and learning things and everything is a bunch of information, and going to college and learning about different cultures; everything is in this form of information rather than an actual experience. Doing a lot of political activism, and feeling the disconnect between the way people treat me -- people fighting together for a cause, and then the disconnect in our personal relationships -- made me want to really focus on what felt true to me, intimate and authentic.

So for me always, autobiography has been the starting point because, there is no way for me to fuck up the way I represent myself. It's so damaging to see the way Asian Americans are portrayed in the movies and in the media here in the States, and so I knew, I'm not going to try to speak for anyone else -- I can speak for myself. My connection into the arts was through ceramics because, not only am I so sick of information, I want to have a truly physical experience, and clay would allow that. What I like about clay is that there is this conversation around utilitarian objects, that when you make a cup, you're actually creating an experience for somebody. Things invested with human labor and human effort get transferred in the use of the object, and that's something that's come to be so near and dear to my heart.

One of the very early projects that I made -- lifetimes ago in 1997 -- was Ceremonial Goblets for Lovers. I grew up with parents who were the product of the '50s, scientific pragmatist thought, and all I had was logic to get me through my life. Anyone knows that will only take you so far before you completely fall apart, and so there's been a need for human touch and intimacy, but a sense of some higher good as well. I went to start an MFA program in studio ceramics, and quickly ditched it, because there's something interesting about being out in the public space. I never lost the need for connection, so I always go back to this piece, my first public piece, where I simply stapled the message, "I love you," on telephone poles around the city. It was a real learning piece for me, to be vulnerable out in public, but also to see a direct connection between me, the maker, and you, whomever. What I learned also is how art can disseminate into the world, because I would go to a party and find one of these slips of paper posted on somebody's mirror, or I would ride my bicycle by here and see someone posing with their camera and taking a selfie. It was really remarkable.

I grew up with this total confusion and frustration around language, where my parents spoke Taiwanese, Mandarin and English at home, but they didn't want me to speak Taiwanese because they thought it was a useless language. They wanted me to speak Mandarin because they thought it was more useful. So I've always had this kind of relationship where I don't really believe in language, because I think of it as a system of social conformity. That's something I've always been exploring, and it's incredible then to go do Snow Poems, and to feel total freedom in poetry, which is not defined by grammar or culture or any kind of logic necessarily.

Moving on from doing my MFA in ceramics, which then was in paper, I went to Roswell, New Mexico, after school. I got into a residency there, and I felt like "all these intellectual ideas and these conceptual ideas that I'm having about art -- they're not going to mean anything to people in Roswell and I'm really interested in doing something that's meaningful to the people of Roswell." In some ways that's the way that I can define my identity as an artist: If I have a purpose for where I am. So I started to look at Roswell and think of different community portraits, and this one I did just by writing the names in the telephone book, connecting them together, in this kind of script that we learned in school -- the correct way of writing. This was actually an incredible project, and meditation, on Roswell where I felt connected to -- everyone! You can imagine, I would see a sign for somebody's barber shop, and I would think, "Oh, I know that person, I wrote their name," or I would meet someone, and

I would know them. So this ended up being 206 pages, and it took six months to write, and it was hung in the Museum of Art so people could come and find their name and see themselves as part of the DNA of Roswell.

Another project I did in Roswell started because on my very first night there, I went to the grocery store -- and in Roswell there are not any Asian people at all -- so this man started following me around the store and looking at me. It was the most horrible and uncomfortable experience to be looked at as a foreigner, as an alien, and then I really understood what Roswell was all about. [laughter] I'm not joking about that.

So I started a project, where I would go up to people and ask them if I could draw a portrait of them, in exchange for them drawing a portrait of my face. And I thought of this as a social service; there's a reason why people are xenophobic in Roswell. I have to let people look at my face because, how can we know each other if we can't even look at each other? That project was really quite painful -- to go up to strangers -- and I thought I would never do that again. Those portraits were then displayed in the museum as well.

I feel like I have this real consciousness of there being an exchange all the time, an interaction and an experience. And in this case, when I drew the portrait of them, I would take a carbon copy; that way I could give them the original and then I could have their drawing.

When I moved to the Bay Area, we were in a restaurant at one point, and my partner at the time noticed that every time we had dinner somewhere there were at least 3 couples meeting for the first time from internet dating. So there was this idea of, "Can we really be intimate through technology?" I ended up doing this portrait exchange through the computer, through a live video conference. So you can see on the picture on the left, that's the gallery where I would call out to people and they would come sit down with me. In a way I had to lure them in -- I think there's something about community art projects where you always lure people in -- but for a real need that I had. I would draw their picture, and I would fax it to them at a fax machine next to the computer, and so they would have it in a matter of seconds. And then they would draw a picture of me, and post it on the gallery wall. There was always this idea of having participants be the artist and be the ones who have their work in the gallery. So on the bottom picture, there's a picture of me. I'm at home and my original drawings are posted on my wall. It's fun to go back to this, and see how similar it is to Snow Poems. How, instead of a window, it's a piece of paper, and someone has the opportunity to express themself just using my face as a mirror. I thought of these as portraits, as a community portrait, just using my face as the mirror.

While I was doing this, I was pregnant. And the day I went into labor, I called and said, "Well I'm not going to be coming in anymore." Then we moved here to Santa Fe, and as a mom with a daughter, and this isolation at home, there was even more need to connect with people. I felt really lost as an artist, and wanted to start working with other people. That's when I started the Cut + Paste Society. Looking back, I wanted to work in a way that was larger than I could even think of for myself, and I wonder, was Cut + Paste Society an excuse for other things, for possibly larger projects, or was it was it a way just to connect. I mean it was all of those things, and it was a way to jump start any kind of creativity that I had. I think that's what collaboration is always, it's getting out of your own habits, your own limitations, and finding something larger.

The idea for Snow Poems came about in some of the early Cut + Paste meetings. We had a show and tell, where people would come and share what they were doing, so we could get to know each other. This woman Rebecca, who was a student at College of Santa Fe at the time, had done her final project, a temporary installation. And she got this temporary snow at Hobby Lobby, and sprayed it in these long, sweeping lines that went from the window down to the floor. Immediately we were so excited, like, "Wow, spray snow, that's so amazing, what can we do with it?" and so there was all this conversation around it. One of the members, Sarah, was teaching at New Mexico School for the Arts, ended up using it in a stencil project with her students, and we continued to think about what we might do with it.

There was the project that Axle Art had done, the Haiku Roadsign Project, that I was blown away by, and I just remember driving up Cerrillos during the summer where there was tons of construction. It was the worst street on earth, and then seeing a poem, and having it melt my heart. So I was looking for something like that again -- Can we bring intimacy to our public space, without having to be really masculine about it, but doing something in a gentle way that can seep into the city?

This is my kitchen window. I moved into this place, and I had put tracing paper on the window so I could still get light, but would still have a little bit of privacy. I think then, the idea of Snow Poems kind of congealed through my body, through my house in this way. Looking back, also, It's so interesting. I watched Wheel of Fortune with my parents for about 15 years because they were learning English idioms from watching that. So I look at these Snow Poems and I think-- Wheel of Fortune. [laughter]

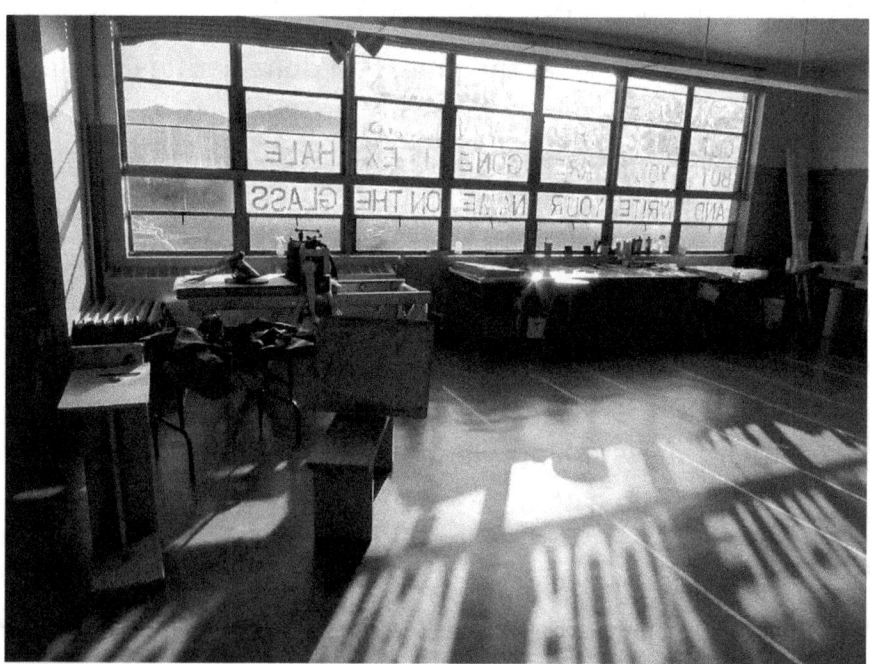

Snow Poems, poem by NMSA Students

I was teaching at New Mexico School for the Arts then, and I got to start the project immediately. There were the windows there, the students who could write the poetry, and could install the poems as well, and it was great. I remember talking with Cristina Gonzalez, the chair of the art department there. I kept trying to find a time when I could present the

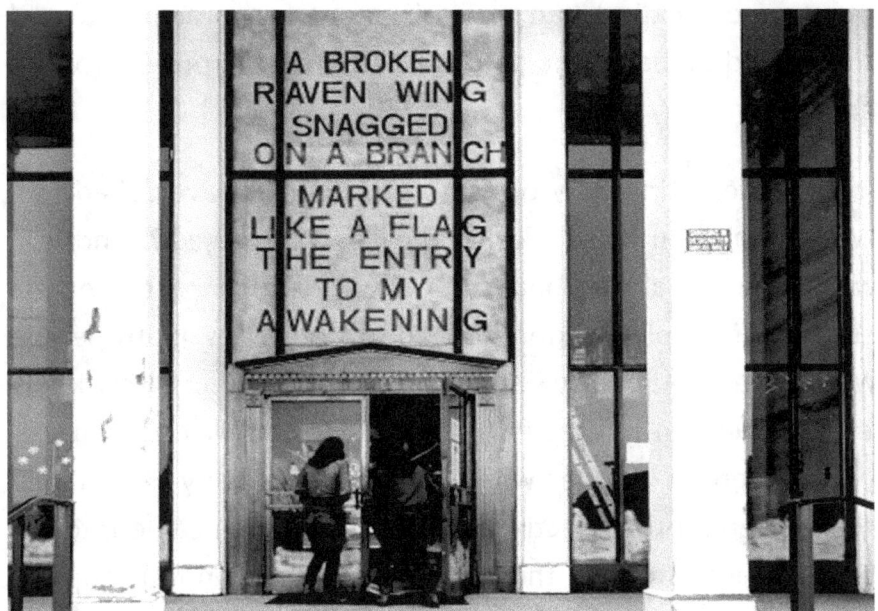

Snow Poems, poem by Michelle Laflamme-Childs

project at a staff meeting -- finally I did that, and she said to me, "Edie, no one's going to help you on this. No one has time. If you want to see it happen, you have to make it happen." And that is really how projects happen.

So this was working with Dr. Monika Cassel's class. That was really great, with the students installing poems, and it all happened in this huge flash. From the very beginning, some of us in Cut + Paste Society knew we wanted to do it around the city, we could see that potential. And we did one window at Margi Gallery -- Kirsten Mundt's window. From this experience of working with the school, and doing the one in the city, it was pretty obvious -- if were going to make it something larger, it was going to take a lot of planning. So Kirsten and I wrote a proposal for SITE Santa Fe's Spread grant, and luckily I had a whole month to practice it, and that ended up being the seed money to do the project for the entire city.

It's so interesting how projects go. People have asked me, "Why didn't you just make it Edie Tsong's project?" and in a way, that was a possibility, but if we were going to get the support of people working on it, I don't know how many people would want to help out on Edie Tsong's project. You know there's such an interesting thing about the way community projects go. I wonder what the real possibility is if it had really been more collective. But once the idea came into my body, I never stopped thinking about it, and I never stopped having the drive to make it happen -- for whatever irrational reason, I knew I had to do it.

I remember when we first won the Spread grant, which was about seven thousand dollars, and we met with Diane Karp, and Michelle Laflamme-Childs who is here today, and we decided we would partner with Santa Fe Art Institute. And I wrote my first budget ever, which was torturous. There's something as an artist that you have to decide -- Do you want to do a project, or do you want to do what the money will let you do? Diane said, "Well you have the money to do fifteen windows." Just thinking of the city, and how fifteen poems could get lost -- In my head it was, "No way, we're going to do at least fifty." I didn't say that, but I knew that, and Diane said, "You know, I've seen artists do this. They always do something beyond what the budget is, and they burn out, and then they can't do it again". That is exactly what happened. I totally burnt out, and it took me over a year to recover -- and I still have really mixed feelings about doing Snow Poems again.

I mean it's a reality. I think it's a strange choice that you have to make. Do you want to go with your heart, or are you going to be realistic and sustainable, and where can both happen? The project continued to grow. I think what I didn't realize as much was that the collaboration was really with the city. That once people knew about the project, people would come forward to me suggesting different things. What I've learned as an artist who always showed at non-profit spaces, you do your own self-promotion. You have to drum up interest. You have to get the word out. All of this is a lot of work. So then it wasn't just the installation, but there was an opening to draw interest, and I want to tell you, I met Joan Logghe in Roswell a few years ago. What a great place to meet someone. She has been a mentor since then, and I feel really lucky that she helped get the word out. Kirsten helped bring in poets from Santa Fe University of Art and Design where she was teaching. Jamie Figueroa, who had studied at The Institute of American Indian Arts, brought in poets from there also, and we ended up having this amazing opening event.

Then there was the idea of: How do we get poems for the windows? We had free poetry workshops, and we had open submissions on the website. We ended up working with interns from Santa Fe University of Art and Design, and from New Mexico School for the Arts, as well.

The process of installing the poems was so laborious, and I had this terror. You know, there are things that you have to do visually so that people don't question what you're doing. Like, if it was sloppy, then it wasn't going to work out, because it would draw attention to that. So people would look at the poems and think that it just took a second to put it up. The one on the left with the scaffolding, that was the largest one. The first image I showed you today, took five people working for five hours, including two hours of setting up scaffolding up and taking the scaffolding down for two other people. It was the most amazing and fun process. We did this during the week after Christmas, and so I will always remember this as the best winter I ever had. Even working with all of the interns -- I was so worried that they would burn out because lining everything up straight and measuring things out, had the feel of doing a standardized test. We would put up a poem, and everyone would be in a daze, but every time we would peel back the letters, there would be these "Ooh"s and "Ahh"s -- and we couldn't believe how beautiful it was. Even though we were doing the work, just being out in the city, it still felt like fairies had put up the poems in the middle of the night. I want to mention, also, that there was a guide map. I don't know if you guys picked one up, but they were free at the different locations. So you could open up the map, and you could visit every single location if you wanted, and then there was every poem on the back as well.

Another way that the project grew in ways that I didn't expect it to -- the poem on the left was at Aaron Payne's Gallery. He had seen the project at New Mexico School for the Arts the year before, and was really in love with it, and wanted a poem on his window. And I thought, "Oh, it's such a tiny window. It's not even going to be significant. It won't even look good", but he was really enthusiastic. So we did the window there, and it was true: In the end, my favorite windows were the tiny ones. There were several cases where different independent businesses could see the value of the project, and drawing attention to their business, and really connecting to the city in a greater way.

On the right, that was The Old Santa Fe Trail Garage, and that was one of the real victories of the project; that poem's by Lauren Camp. I remember from the beginning, I'd wanted to see a poem on that window because I walked by that building every day; it's this retro-garage, and it's just gorgeous. I approached him several times about having a poem on his window, and he said, "Oh yeah, maybe my granddaughter can write something." Then as it came closer to needing to do the Snow Poem, he started to try to avoid me. I got really worried, because I needed to see a poem on that window. Then one day I went in at lunchtime, and his friend was sitting there. I re-explained the project, and the friend was really enthusiastic about it, and because of that, the garage owner reluctantly decided to do it. In the end, he was this total convert, because so many of his customers commented on it and were really excited about it. So that was one of the real victories. I think there's this really beautiful way of working with Cut + Paste, that being moms, we all

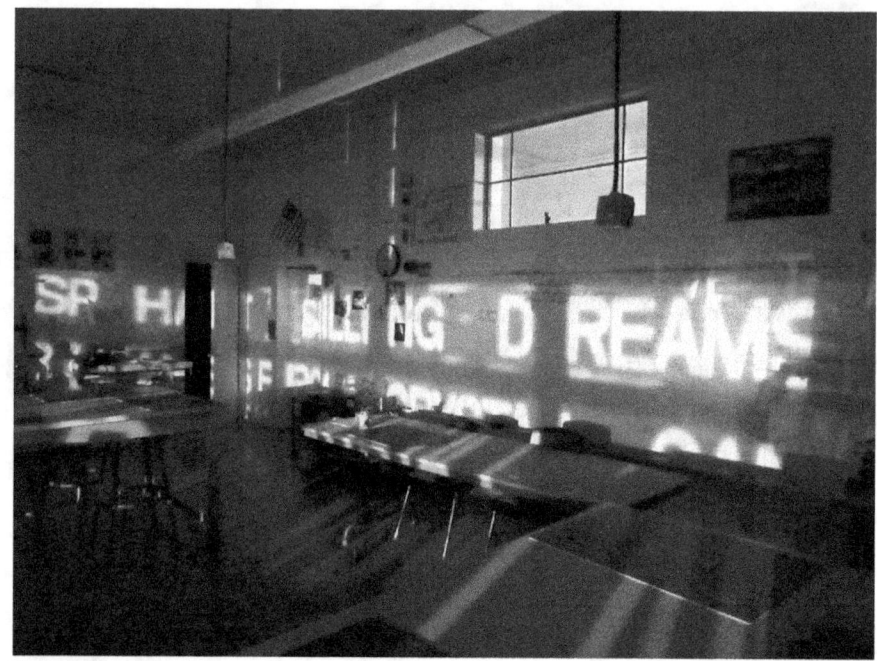

Snow Poems, poem by Jacob Sisneros

wanted to see poems at the schools where our kids go, so Katie McCauley, who had never taught poetry before, went into three classes in 3rd grade at Carlos Gilbert Elementary and taught poetry workshops, and we put up three Snow Poems there. Kirsten taught at Turquoise Trail, where her daughter was going to school, and then I got my daughter's teacher at Wood Gormley to teach a poetry workshop as well. Katie's husband, who had a window washing business, ended up volunteering about $2,000 worth of window cleaning for the project.

I forgot to mention, at the beginning poetry reading that was the opening for the whole project, I had this feeling like I was getting married to the city. I had never had to order chairs before. You know the way you imagine people might order chairs for a wedding, and then rather than ordering a cake, I was getting the Cut + Paste members to bake cookies. It felt like my marriage to the city. And in the course of that poetry reading, I realized why Snow Poems was happening in Santa Fe. There are so many poets. There are so many artists here. It was like the creativity was just naturally seeping out the windows. I think there's this kind of fated-ness that I had, that whatever strange work I did, including being a waitress and working for caterers, these were all the skills needed to combine with the City of Santa Fe to make Snow Poems happen. It was also a way to just play, and so we ended up having Night of Illumination as a closing ceremony, where we asked people to keep the lights on at night, and Molly Sturges, who just spoke, led a Snow Poems Choir, which was amazing. People took excerpts from poems for this choir. You'll see in the picture here, there were walking tours. Jamie Figueroa led a tour, and Michelle led a tour.

I love the idea that Snow Poems expresses. Everything in poetry and this city is a book. Every part a page. I love Santa Fe. I love poetry.

The day we went it snowed. I have a fear of downtown but this time I wasn't alone or scared. The snow made it innocent again. The simplicity of the poems, of the fresh fallen snow. The optimism that we read said that poetry is an impractical curative. It keeps me afloat. It gets a message across, even if it just be a smile. Isn't that some sort of activism?

So Snow Poems - the full cycle - ended this January in printing the Snow Poems postcard book. In the beginning we had the idea to make a book of all the poems with images of the windows, but then Sydney Cooper had this great idea, "Why don't you make a postcard book?" I searched all over the Santa Fe Plaza to find this correct kind of book that I wanted to make, that I had seen before. I couldn't find a single postcard book like that, but my parents who had traveled a lot, they had a postcard book from the seventies that was this accordion style. I ended up having my mom send it to me, and that's what I used to bring to the printer.

I feel like everything about this project comes from home, and that's what art is, really. It's not looking outside of you but looking to your own needs. There's something beautiful I learned about Snow Poems also, that in gathering people, as we are today, it's always an incredible moment -- we're here together for some reason and it's not just to have wine and drinks. It's not to talk about the weather, but there's something about art and social engagement that brings us together, and it's important to recognize that, because it will take us somewhere else.

Another thing is, working with Cut + Paste, we've been having these different conversations around creativity. There's one tomorrow at Saint Francis Auditorium, but just that the individual voice is medicine for the collective, that what I need is what other people need, and it's not a selfish act, to express myself. It's actual medicine.

Thank you. [applause] Questions?

Audience member:

One thing that struck me is, from the beginning you have a background, however fleeting, as a ceramicist, and from the beginning this idea of handmade aesthetic. And yet when we think about social practice or public art we tend to think about scale. I was wondering -- you ended with this postcard book, which again is small in scale and handmade. I was wondering if you could maybe address this idea, for you anyway, what the relationship is between say the handmade, and social practice.

Edie Tsong:

I think for me what the handmade is, is the intimacy. And so it goes back to the idea of things invested with human energy. They emit human energy. Even though we did that postcard book which is mass produced, it was still small scale, offset printing, it wasn't digital printed. It was almost like this handmade book project, working with a small printer. I just want to give a shout out to Tom Kirby, who helped us print it and who passed away a few weeks ago. Another thing in ceramics is, people were talking about if you throw a pot with an electric wheel, you make an electric pot. If you throw a pot with a kick wheel it's a different kind of pot, and the thing that I'm really interested in, in what I do, is bringing intimacy, and this quality of being human together. I've always had this distrust of things being too large and too glossy. Am I answering your question?

Audience member:

Yes... in relation to the general concept of social practice which is an umbrella for a lot of activity. But a lot of that activity, particularly historically, has been conceptual. And right from the beginning with Cut + Paste meetings, with the person who sprayed the snow, I was struck all through this -- the people working and the people that were bought into this, even though there were fifty or sixty poems, pretty ambitious activity -- all through this, there's this personal, handmade touch to everything that goes into it at the same time. In the way that you recruited the poets and students. That's what I was thinking about.

Edie Tsong:

I think that's my natural inclination as an artist. I think for social projects, it runs the gamut, it really does, but for me, intimacy and the quality of interaction is at the heart of what I do. I think it's so interesting to look at a project like One Million Bones by Naomi Natale. All these bones are handmade, but then there's a million of them, so it's this whole different scale. There's still that quality of being human. Some of my favorite projects come back to Harell Fletcher and Miranda July, "Learning to Love You More," where basically, it's letting a human being have a voice. There are these projects on-line where you can tell a story about a scar you have and there are 20 stories uploaded about your scar. Projects really run the gamut and for me, the handmade is something that is so important, and to fight against this mass produced shiny world.

Audience Member:

I have a comment. I think that I told you this before but I'm not sure. There were two amazing experiences that happened as a result of Snow Poems, for me. The first one was I, like probably a lot of people, get very wrapped up in my regular daily life. Full time job, part time job, two children -- just all of the things that make life crazy -- and one Saturday or Sunday, one of the kids had a birthday party, and I live out in Eldorado and we had forgotten about it and we were rushing. It was manic and I was pissed off that we had to come into town and go to this stupid birthday party and I had forgotten a present.

I was freaking out and I was angry and yelling at the kids and we get to play and there's a Snow Poem on the window. It was like that. It took me out of that ridiculous whirlwind of anger that I had frothed up into, and just for a second it was quiet and I saw. It transformed that moment into, "I'm going to a birthday party, for a beautiful little child!" Like, get over yourself! That interaction with that piece was massive, in that moment.

Edie Tsong:

That little window that was at Play. Nina kept on begging me to do a Snow Poem there and I said, "Oh but it's so little. It only fits 11 letters" -- and it did end up being another one of the huge successes in this project.

Audience Member:

And of course seeing my own, on this huge state building -- being the person who wrote that giant one that you guys spent all that time doing.

Edie Tsong:

And then you could see that poem from a mile away. It was amazing!

Audience Member:

It was an incredible experience to see my words like that, and it was very moving for me too, and very empowering, because as a poet I'd hidden my work from public view for my entire life until I was in my forties, and so to have that piece up there that publicly, was a huge thing for me, so, thank you.

Edie Tsong:

Oh man, you're so welcome.

We did a blind curation for the poems for the windows, and it was kind of based on how long the poem was and how many letters would fit on a window, and, the first time I ever came to Santa Fe I went to James Kelly Gallery and I was like -- I love this gallery. I would love to show here -- and it was interesting that my poem was chosen for James Kelly Gallery. That's not the way I thought I would be showing there, but I did get to show there. [laughter] The poems changed the city for me and we knew, in the beginning, the reason why we're doing this is to bring intimacy to our public spaces, but we couldn't have guessed how profound it would be and it would feel in our bodies while we walked around the city. To me it's so beautiful to see that you don't have to be an architect, you don't have to be a city planner, to change the space where you live. You can be an artist.

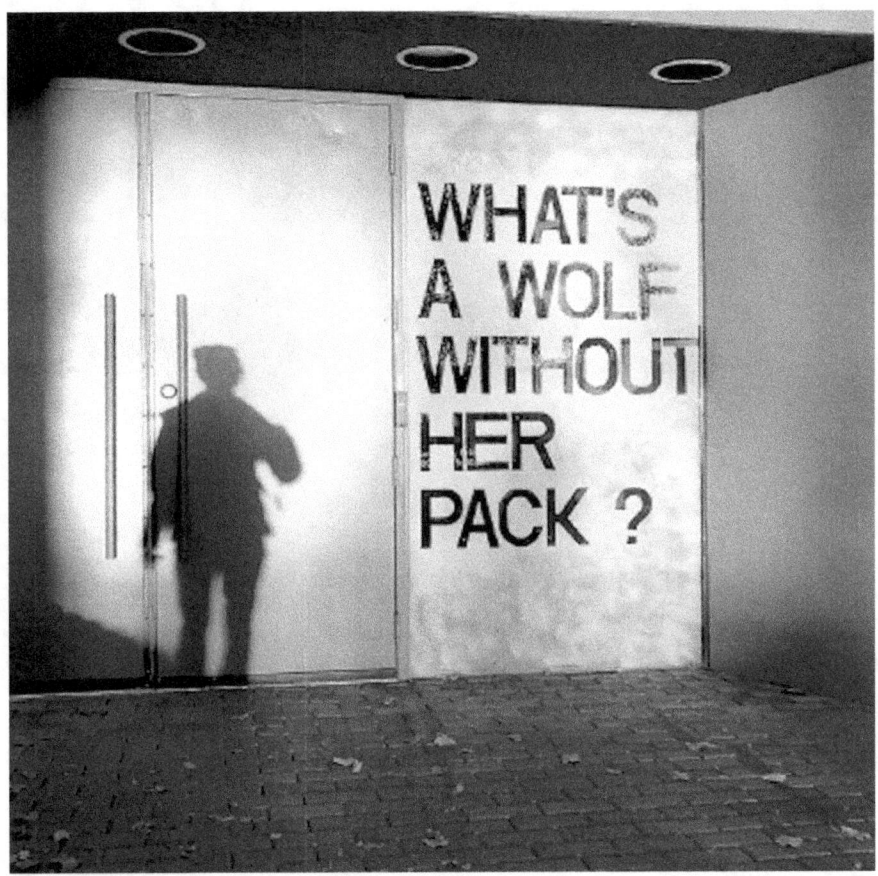

Snow Poems, poem by Karen Dodier

Bobbe Besold
Dominique Mazeaud

RIVERS RUN THROUGH US

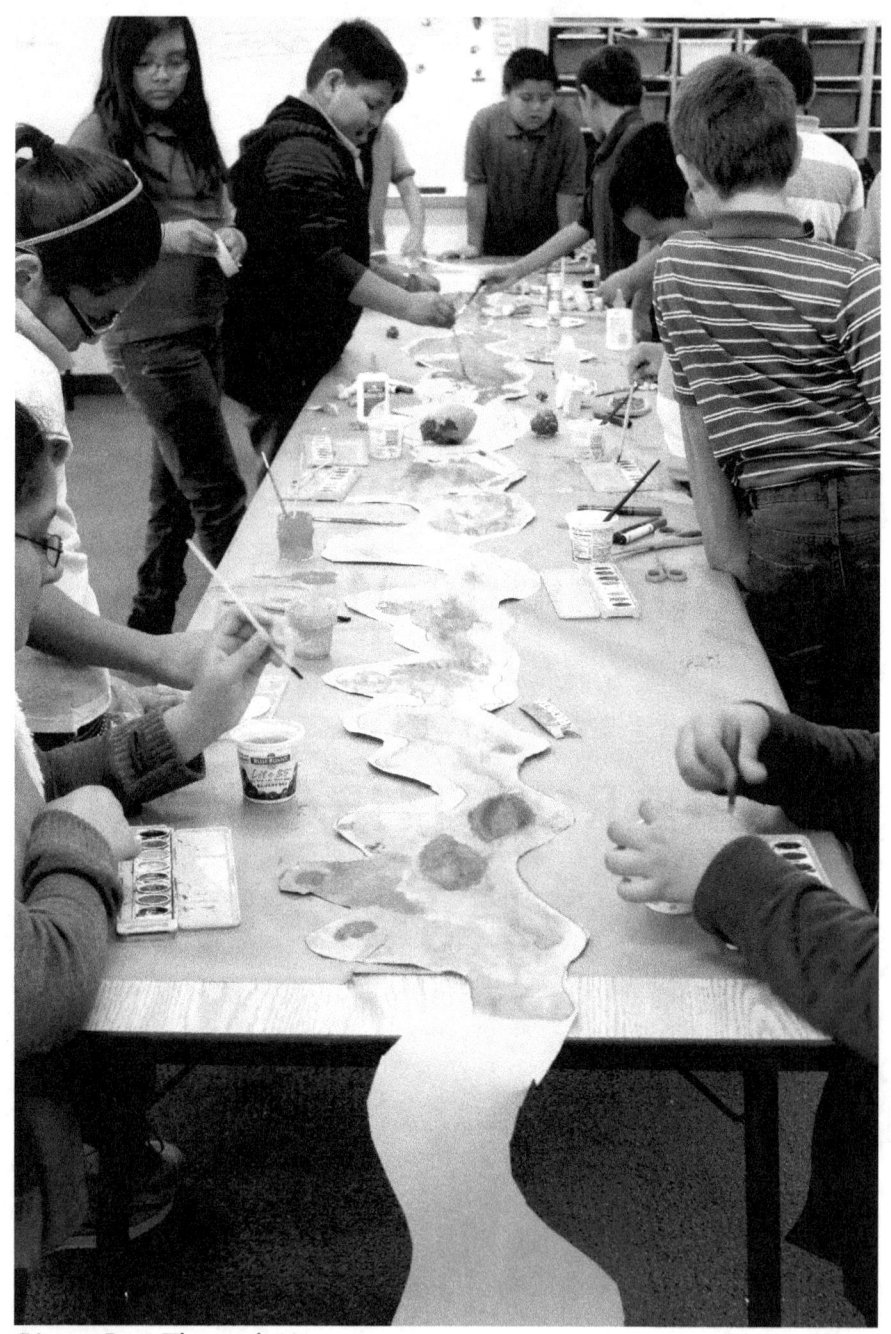

Rivers Run Through Us

Dominique Mazeaud:

I think I need to give you the context for why I am sitting in front of you, because I didn't start as an artist. I started as a gallerist. I was in New York, and kept thinking, "There is more to what I need to do with art." That lead me, eventually, to some very powerful experiences, which revealed to me that I was here to find out, what is the spiritual in art, in our time. That's a big mouthful of an introduction but I always put it this way, because that's what I heard through that experience. That was in 1979, so I have been carrying that answer for 35 years, and I thought first, because I had been a gallerist, that I would find it through other artists; but then the little voice kept talking to me and said "Join the ranks!"

This happened in a very extraordinary way. I was by the Rio Grande in 1986, with a Native American friend actually, and we were trying to take a walk by the river, and it was trashed everywhere. It really was a bad scene. At that time I really got in touch with what was happening to the earth, and to the waters, and my heart literally broke. At that moment I had another little instruction, and got the idea that I was going to do this project, "The Great Cleansing of the Rio Grande." which I did for seven years every month going to the river. Starting with the Santa Fe River and walking my way to the Rio Grande, which I never did reach, because it takes a long time to clean the river, picking up every month where we left off last month. And the river set me on many adventures.

Sometimes it takes you a long time to realize your dream, and my dream was to walk to the Rio Grande -- which as you know, the Santa Fe River meets the Rio Grande in Cochiti Pueblo. Here comes Bobbe, some three years ago or so, who said, "Oh, you know, you know we can pick up from here" -- we can go back and forth.

Bobbe Besold:

I want to give you a little bit of background about how I came into working with water. I've always been an artist, or known that I wanted to be an artist, since I was three. So I'm one of those people, but when I was in the 7th grade I was asked to do a project about something in our community. I grew up on Long Island in New York, and the house that I grew up in was a suburban house, and there was a sand mine back there. If you walk in the streets of New York City and you look down at the sidewalk, you'll see that there's seashells, there's fossilized shells and there's little bits of shell in there, and that's the sand that came from the neighborhood that I grew up in.

This sand mine was gradually encroaching on the forest and the pond that I used to skate on in the winter. It was eating it's way closer and closer to my neighborhood. I went down and I did a drawing -- a watercolor -- of this building where the sand comes in -- it's sorted and comes out on the other side. I wrote about the sand mine and what was happening. It was my first piece of art and activism. I believe that from that moment, just about everything that I've ever done has been formed, in some way -- by my need to express myself through art -- also my need to express the pain that I feel, and the grief and the joy as well, and the beauty of the earth.

In terms of coming to water -- well, I want to talk a little about how I met Dominique; I worked for some time at the Center for Contemporary Arts, here, as a curator and preparator, and Dominique came in and was bringing an exhibit that she had curated, called Revered Earth. There were many amazing artists, one of whom was Betsy Damon, who continues to do incredible work with water. That was our first meeting, and we were within the same community and on the periphery of each other for many years. I was teaching a class at the Community College called Art and Activism, and Dominique was working on these really interesting projects where she was collecting children's shoes -- the first pair which she found in the Santa Fe River. So I invited her to come to the class to present to my students. She did this amazing project, where the shoes were there on the ground, and then the students were there, and Dominique was there and she spoke, and it opened up something for the students, but it also opened up my relationship with this woman. From that point on we began doing more and more projects together.

We did a project in Albuquerque for the LAND/ART show, in 2009 or 2010. Dominique had been working with The Women in Black, and then she created this from that offshoot. She created The Women in White -- The Water Weaving Women. Do you want to talk about that?

Dominique Mazeaud:

Yes, there were 60 of them. I had a dream where I was walking with a crown of 60 lit candles. This was in 2005, when I was involved with activism, and one of my issues has been the nuclear issue. At that time it was the 60th anniversary of the bombing of Hiroshima, and the number 60 has been very important to me, and I've used it, because I love symbols and 60 is the symbol for time. When I first used it at a performance at SITE Santa Fe, it was 2005. Now I feel we are so much more oppressed -- time feels even more like we need to do things, more quickly, and so that's why I've been using 60 Water Weaving Women and 60 in different pieces...

Bobbe Besold:

I curated a show at the State Capitol building and Dominique created a piece with the 60 women but these were the 60 Water Weaving Women. Talk a little about that.

Dominique Mazeaud:

Even though my background was art -- I worked with all the well known abstract expressionists, I worked with Motherwell, I worked with de Kooning, all these guys -- but when it was revealed to me that I was an artist, I said, "I'm doing art for the earth." I let go of the whole art thing, I never promoted my project. But I feel when your heart really leads you to speaking for the earth, you're supported. I didn't promote myself, and then this critic heard about my project, and before I knew it, it was written about. When I first said I was an artist, I always felt people were putting me on a pedestal, and other folks were down below. For me it's not the world that I'm dreaming of, and so that's why we're still working to be "heart-ists." That's what I want on my calling card, because I feel we all have that within us. Whether we put poems all over our city, and we work in the river, or we are chefs, or a masseur or mechanic; if it's your passion... Anyway, I'm going off the river. The river keeps you meandering, and then also you learn to go with the flow.

Bobbe Besold:

Dominique did an amazing performance piece in the Rotunda at the Sate Capitol building, with all these women dressed in white, in collaboration with Elizabeth Wiseman from Theater Grottesco. Madi Sato also sang and taught us a piece to go with it. It was really powerful and beautiful, to have all of these women in the space, revering water. We all were carrying water with us.

We continued on that theme; We did a piece for LAND/ART along one of the ditches in Albuquerque where we used the same theme -- a call for women to wear white, and again used the 60 women, and so there were women from Albuquerque and women from here who drove down for this. Dominique and I were walking along the canal talking about what to do and I just saw, "everybody's going to bring a bucket from home, the regular little bucket that you have at your house, and everyone will carry that in on their head," and so that's what we had. It's this wonderful image of all these women in white but everybody's got a different color bucket on their head, and at one point we had ropes tied to each of the handles of the bucket. Women threw them into the canal, dragged some water up and so on.

Dominique Mazeaud:

It was a way to connect with women in Africa who walk ten kilometers to get some water. For me there's such a connection between our lives and our art. For example the piece I developed at the Rotunda, we used pitchers in that piece, and that came from a ritual I've been doing for many years. I have a pitcher by my sink and I do a little kitchen ceremony by collecting the cold water until I get to the hot water, and I use that water to water my plants, and put in the birdbath. That gesture, which I did for years, was the seed. You don't have to look, it's just the connection between art and life. That's why at this point I don't really write about this split of art and life. My answer is life as art, and connecting the two, art, life, spirit, more and more. I know maybe artists don't talk about spirit, but to me, all this work everybody here is doing is very much what I see as the spiritual in art in our time. Some people are uncomfortable with that term, but for me that's what I'm concerned with.

Bobbe Besold:

So I'm in alignment with that one, very much so... I guess I should give you a little piece about myself, which is that I am primarily a visual artist -- that's what I studied -- but I've also along the way done a lot of performance and work in theater, and did design for theater, costume and video, so there's a lot of layers. I believe that there should be no limits to what media we decide to use. If we need it, we can figure it out.

After the project at the Capitol building, Dominique and I were talking and I said- You know I heard that the name for Santa Fe in Tewa is "Poge," and that it means water place. Where was the water? Where was it? Dominique said, "I heard that there was a spring at the Inn of the Anasazi." So that led to a conversation where we began studying where these springs were. We went to the history library, and then we started walking the Santa Fe River together, and then invited women to come and walk in the river with us as well. Basically we decided we were going to do this walk. We're going to follow the river to the Rio Grande, we're going to do that.

Dominique Mazeaud:

We're going to show you the film. We are a collaboration with Valerie Martinez, and you're going to see the three of us walking the whole river, which was really the performance that started this project. Which was totally engaging the community, but we felt we had to start with this very strong performance of five days walking, 54 miles.

see video at www.evolvingintentionsinpublicart.org

[applause]

Bobbe Besold:

Before we do go on to a little section of questions I would like everybody to stand up.

Thinking about what you just saw, or some influence of what you just saw. I would like you to move in some way -- all of you to move, however that comes to you. Just move.

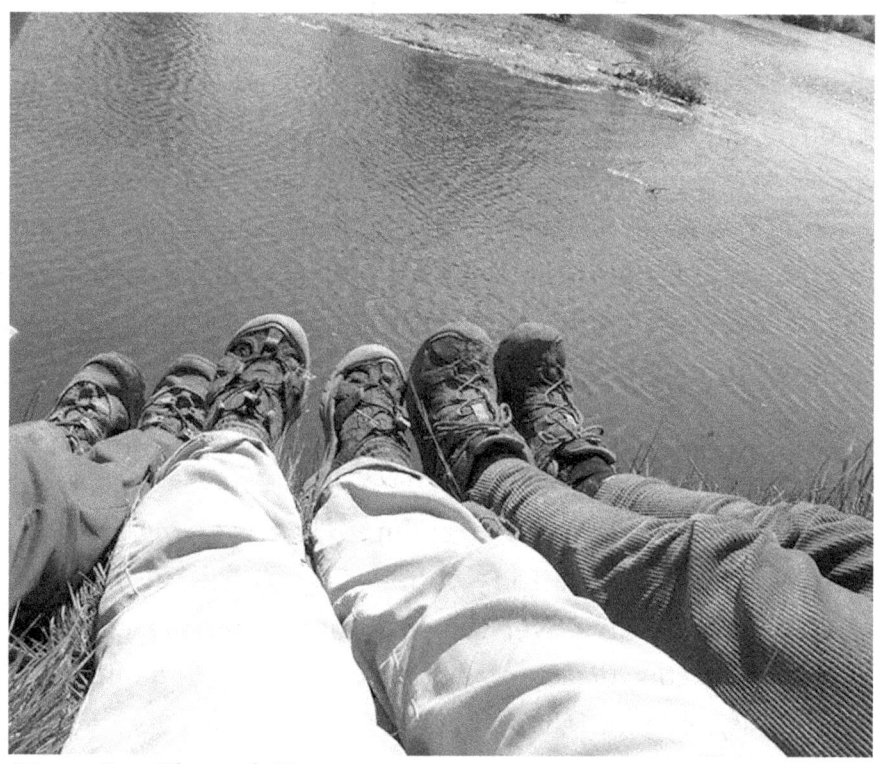
Rivers Run Through Us

You can move in place, dance around. Anything you want to do. If you need to close your eyes you can do that.

Each of you will do this. I want you to say, briefly, a few words, something that comes to your head about this.

"Continuum," "water is not free," "connective", "connecting," "life energy," "the earth," "blue, brown," "living," "treasure water," "fresh," "I don't know," "water," "elements", "energy," "we're all made of water," "ceremony," "wet", "footsteps," "dry," "earth", "rain," "cracked", "footsteps."

Bobbe Besold:

Beautiful. Thank you. Questions, thoughts?

Audience Member:

Were you able to obtain permission to walk through the upper watershed?

Bobbe Besold:

It is forbidden to walk up there. It's been closed for 80 years, or over 80 years now, so we approached the city because they have the clout. We met with the mayor, we met with many different people. We had to go in with a couple of folks from the city that day. They wouldn't let us walk down from the ski basin, which is what we wanted to do, and just start at Santa Fe Lake, which is the beginning of the Santa Fe River. Because they knew, and we knew, it was going to take longer. A really long, long first day, and we might have to spend the night in the upper watershed, and no, you don't do that. We drove in by truck to the very, very end of the road that you can go, and past both dams and the reservoirs, and hiked in with Dale Lyons, and two women from the Watershed Association came with us as well. Dale had never been up in there, so he didn't really know where he was going. We did a lot of bushwhacking that day, and our goal was to reach a place where there's a little tributary that comes into the Santa Fe River. We didn't quite make it there. We got amongst some of these 80-year-and-older trees, which was incredible, and a lot of wildlife, a lot of amazing beavers and things like that.

Audience Member:

Can you tell a little bit about how you engaged the community around your walk, because there's some footage of discussion, and people joining you, so I would like to know more about that.

Dominique Mazeaud:

We discovered a lot. It's two different worlds, from the city through the farming communities, and the ranchers and then down to Cochiti. A big part of a project like this, the way to connect with community, is to really respect, listen, share what we're intending to do. We got permission from everybody, and that took a very long time. Cochiti Pueblo took months, maybe even six months. To me I see this kind of work as weaving the web, and I was a weaver one time, as Edie was a potter. We really forged relationships with people, and we continued. We worked in the schools, also, we worked at the New Mexico School for the Arts. We met with private land owners up near the Audubon. A very big part is to really listen to the people, and we found ourselves, in a way, a go-between with the folks from here, like the environmentalists, and the ranchers.

Bobbe Besold:

This project is a restoration of the river, but it's also a restoration of the community, and that includes not just the human beings, but also the plants and the animals, all of the beings that live along the river. That is an essential part of our landscape. The other element of engaging the community, was the fact that we also recorded people's stories; we met with as many people as we could who live along the river, and also invited artists and others to meet us. As you saw -- there were a few little clips in there. Molly came and did a beautiful choir to San Isidro Crossing. Each time there was a group, like the group of home schoolers near the upper watershed, there was this energy rippling out of that little piece -- of what you can do as seed planters, which is what each of us are. We go out every day and carry this enthusiasm for the project, or ideas, and we talk to others and we plant these seeds.

The Rivers Run Through Us is a vehicle for us to speak to many, many different kinds of people -- a great diversity of community -- and also be able to advocate for these things in a way that we do through listening. That's a huge part of what we do, listening. There's a group that formed, in part because of our project, called The Santa Fe River Traditional Community Collaborative. They meet once a month in La Cienega, and it's the lower part of the river, where you saw water running again. And I'd like to hear from somebody here, just quickly -- why is the Santa Fe River, as Val said, wet up here, and dry down there, and then wet again? Why? Does somebody know?

Audience Member:

The wastewater treatment plant.

Bobbe Besold:

That's where the water comes in, so why is the middle part dry?

Audience Member:

The water is in our pipes, in the city, instead of in the river.

Bobbe Besold:

Exactly, it goes into our homes. So the damns stop the water. It's piped out and when those damns were originally built, they were designed to not allow any water whatsoever into the Santa Fe River. At that time, it ruined the farming community in Agua Fria Village. It destroyed the agriculture which this community depended upon a great deal.

The film "Damnation" is coming here to CCA. It is a fundraiser for the Gila River. We're involved in kind of a loose way with that, organizing that event for the Gila. Some of you may know, some of you may not know, that river is threatened. It's the one un-damned river in New Mexico and in a large part of North America. It's very important that we save this river -- I cannot express to you more. So come, October 22nd at CCA. Thank you.

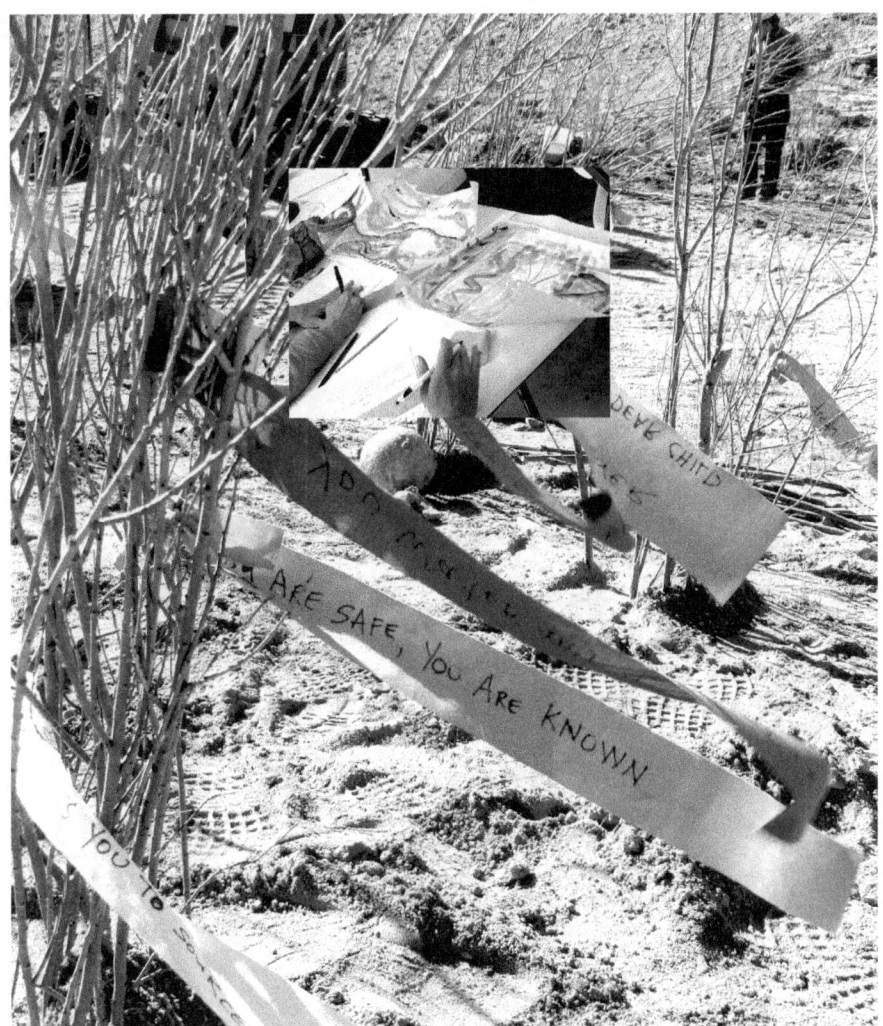

Rivers Run Through Us

Christy Hengst

BIRDS IN THE PARK

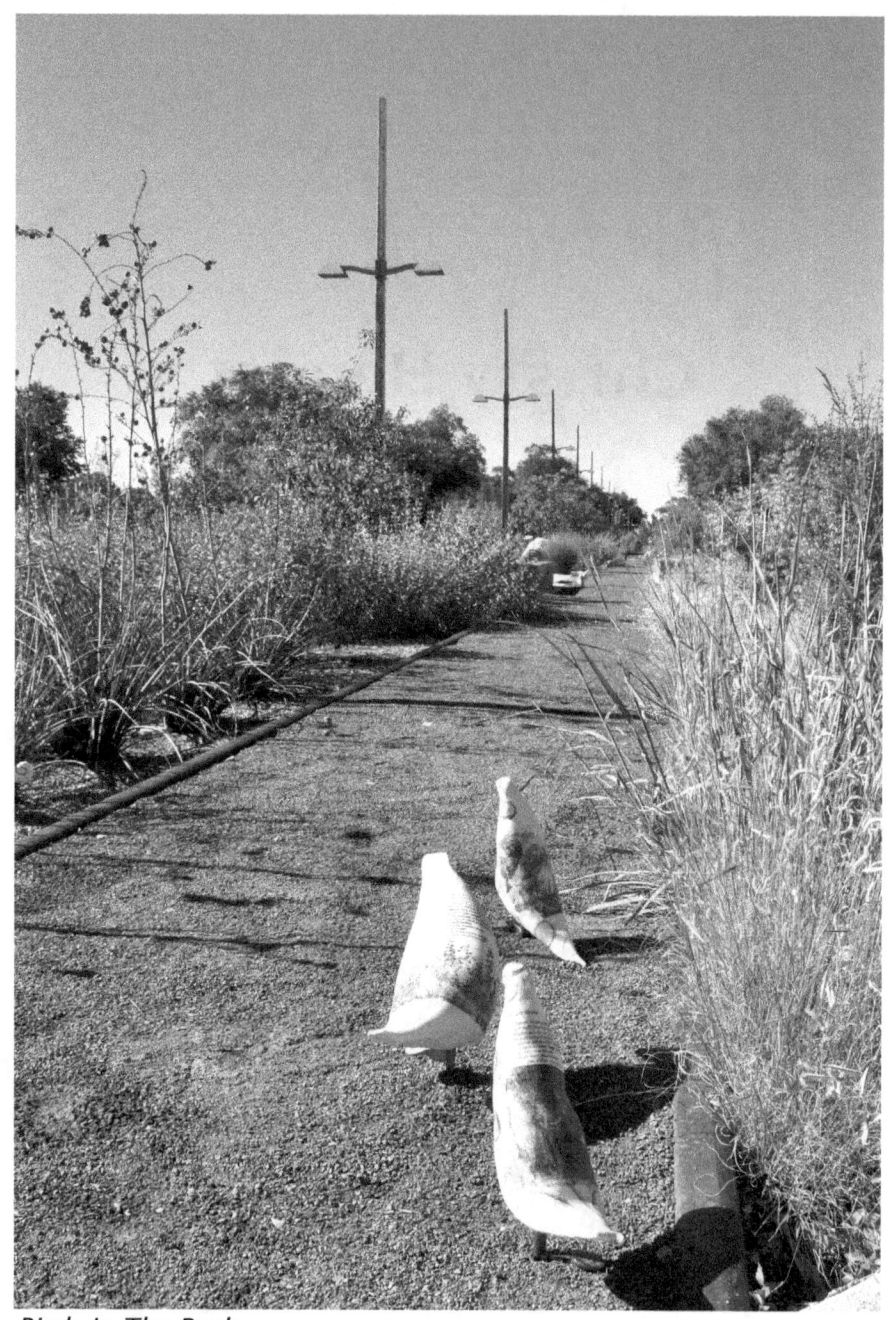

Birds In The Park

Christy Hengst:

I'm going to talk a little bit about a project that I did called 'Birds in the Park'. I started it in 2008 and depending on how you think about it, it went on for about four to six years.

Basically it started with me discovering that I could print onto porcelain while it was still wet, and create three-dimensional pieces with a printed slab. I was printing with cobalt through silkscreen, and using text and image. That's something that I had been doing for a while on flat tiles, but it was something new when I realized I could form pieces that were more like sculpture. Those pieces, at first I thought of as seed pods, but they started to look more and more like birds.

When I was first doing it, I guess I was still thinking in terms of work that might be shown indoors, and I was working with images and text from the lead up to the war with Iraq. I'd saved newspapers from that time -- I was really in shock about it all, that this country had agreed to go to war in that way. Content-wise, it started to change a little bit, as basically I had two lines going. I had this line going that was more imagery and stories about war, writings from a Vietnam vet here in town, and all these newspaper articles and photographs. Then I had another line going that was more like family history -- documents, recipes, love letters, poetry that was meaningful to me, and photos of the kids. I was keeping them separate, and of course as soon as I realized that I was keeping them separate, I realized that was actually, in some way what this was all about -- putting them on the same page.

I started to do that with some of the content. I'd basically make transparencies, and then make silkscreens from those transparencies, and they can start out as any kind of document.

Format-wise, when I started to do this -- like so many projects I have heard about today, they develop completely organically, not a fully formed idea at all in the beginning. All I knew was I started to want to see these pieces outside, or in public, and I started to experiment with that. So this is here at the Farmers Market. [laughing] -- with the idea that I would hide some birds around. It's funny because looking back, I think, "What was I thinking?" They're so high up, nobody even noticed that there were birds up there, but if they did they obviously wouldn't be able to read what was on the backs.

But it was just my way of starting to feel it out, and find my own way through trying things. I did have one group of birds, that day at the Farmers Market, that I just put out in the front, in the gravel. My husband, who is a blacksmith, had helped me to make some stands for them --- and I like what happened with those. Obviously, now people could walk amongst them and could read them. And that is the way it started.

Pretty quickly then, talking with friends, I started to get the idea, Oh okay, I think I'm going to take these birds around to a lot of different places, and I'm going to set them up -- at first it was completely anonymous -- I'm going to set them up secretly, at the break of dawn. Get up there, and basically have them all set up so where there was nothing before, all of a sudden there was something. And it would be something that people would come across in the middle of their daily lives. Not a situation where you go planning to have an art experience, like a museum or a gallery, but where there's just suddenly something odd, and it may break your stride. It may, possibly, open some window of thinking about things differently.

This is at the Tune Up Cafe.

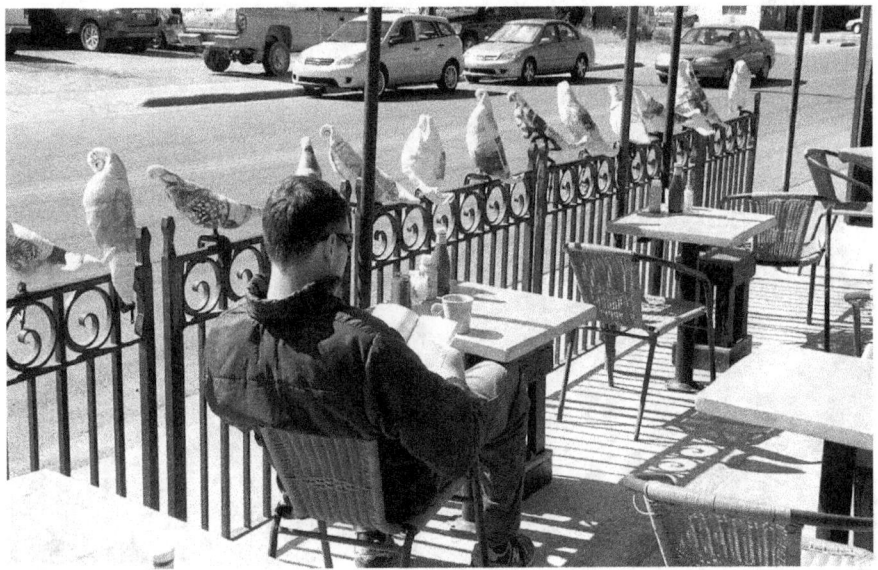

Birds In The Park

So I started to make a list of different places that I would like to see them. Also for totally selfish reasons, just wanting to actually see them in different places. I mean, these are porcelain! Fragile pieces, and to see them in all these different locations was in itself very gratifying for me. Just sensually, I really liked it.

I started to talk with the Santa Fe Arts Commission, and

they helped me to set up some of these locations. Like we were talking in the beginning of these sessions this morning with Matthew, there definitely were some places where I got permission, and some places where I did not, and some places where it was a little bit of a gray area.

Here's Frenchy's Field.

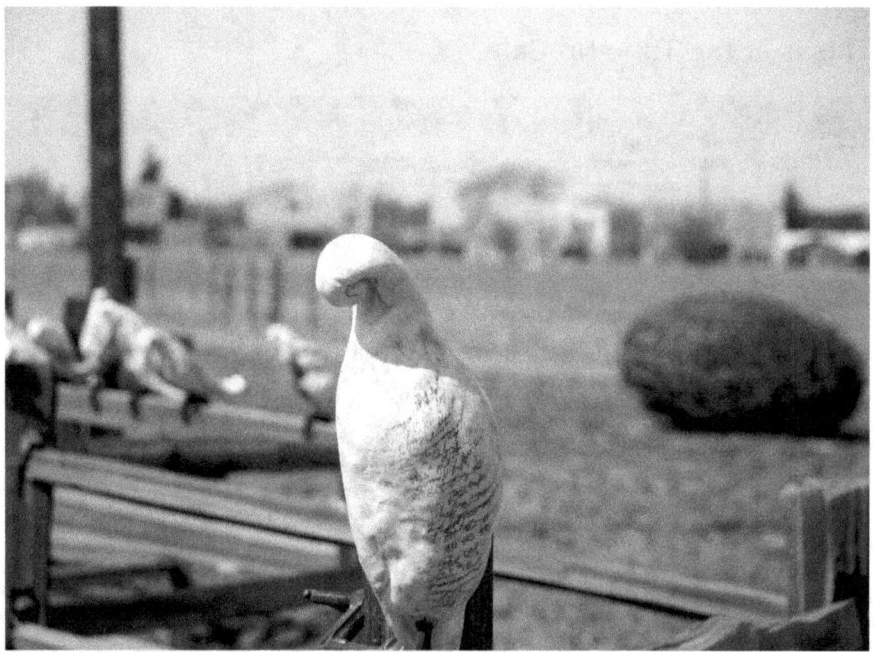

Birds In The Park

Most of the places in Santa Fe, I actually got some kind of permission, where I did talk with somebody, but later that changed sometimes.

This is at the Convention Center, before those fish were there. It's interesting that we had the same idea. This is a spiral of birds.

Like I said, at the beginning it was completely anonymous. I would set them up really early, actually with a friend who was also a mother. The birds were wrapped in all kinds of old clothes for transport, cloth diapers -- clean diapers! -- and all kinds of different things, whatever we could find because we needed a lot of them. I kept making more and more birds. I would set them up, and then I would be unobtrusively nearby for the day. Because they were totally temporarily set, and they were fragile and could be walked away with. And also, because, of course, I went through a lot of work for it -- I wanted to see what happened!

What happened was, of course, a lot of people just walked straight by and didn't pay any attention... or maybe they would notice that actually that flock wasn't moving... and then some of those people would go to investigate further. And some of those people -- I have to admit it was a relatively small percentage of the people -- but some of the people, did in fact did get involved, and start to read, look around, and wonder what this was. And later I found out, when I started talking to people, that they did start to think about the content that was on these birds.

So that was City Hall, Railyard, Santa Fe Art Institute, which was really fun. Lots of support from the people over there.

Friends and family helped. My kids when they were younger. Look at how cute they are!

We were going to go to San Diego to visit a friend, and decided to bring the birds, and wow, was that fun. To set the birds up on the beach, and have the waves wash over them... of course, lots of people saw them on the beach, and I just really loved that. Helmut made these bases really strong so that some of them were actually down in the waves, and ended up underwater when the tide came up.

In some ways this was all still the infancy of the project, because I was starting to develop a format, and I was starting to build my content, but one of the major pieces was actually still not quite there yet because I was really hanging back in terms of interaction.

Here they are.... one of those birds is real... [laughter]

The seagulls were super inquisitive -- in terms of what type of bird is most inquisitive. I would say seagulls.

We started to go to other places. This was in New Orleans, in a sculpture garden. I'm not going to show you all the places they landed -- they landed in seventy-something different places, and it became international.

Washington D.C. was one of the places where I met the most people, and by this point, I was starting to talk with people, and some of those conversations started to feel like that was actually a real part of the project, not an adjunct aspect of it.

The whole thing about permission. I had thought ahead about this, because obviously at the National Mall... I had tried to get a permit and they said: "There's no art allowed on the Mall," except for very specific festivals. I had gone back and forth with the park ranger about this, and she was really

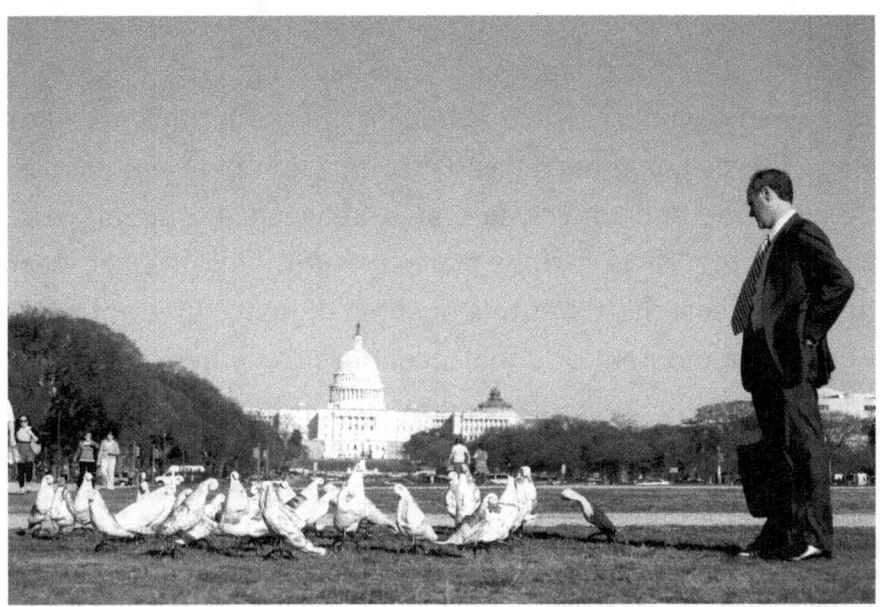

Birds In The Park

adamant. I had basically given up, and then revisited it when somebody said, "You know, it's all about language in D.C. and one thing that's for sure allowed on the National Mall is free speech." So I reapplied, and I said, "I am wanting to do a small, and actually very quiet, political demonstration." [laughter]

I got the permit -- I was really glad I had it when those police showed up -- and it was packed with hundreds of people on this day. And all kinds of stuff came up, but a lot about... You know, nobody's "for war"... but 'how wars start' was a big topic, and the conversations went in all different directions.

One of the things I'm reflecting about -- what I thought worked with this project, what didn't work, what was different from my expectations, in terms of how it turned out -- is that I think that at the beginning I thought that I was going to be changing minds... a little bit, or I would at least be suggesting things about paths that were not so fruitful for us to go on, in terms of starting a war, basically. I don't know if I changed anybody's mind about that. I don't think so. But what did really happen is actual connection between people, between me and others, and also between the people who were there. Conversations started, and I think that, at least in some cases, there was this opening of just a different point of view... a moment of unbalance, possibly, where you come across this thing, you don't know what it is.

One of my big inspirations has been Robert Irwin, and a project he actually never did, but I love. It was called Tilted Squares, and it was on the grassy quad at a university, and he basically proposed to divide the grass into squares in some places, and slightly tilt some of them up. Like build them up with dirt, and have it be like these tiny ramps. I think that one of the reasons they didn't go for it was that it would be really complicated for the lawn mowers, so they never actually did the project. But that idea of stimulating an imbalance in your normal perception, that then creates a possible moment of opening of consciousness, almost like you have become aware of your own perception, your own consciousness. I love that idea. I love when it happens to me.

This was an immigration demonstration in D.C. and lots going on. The birds visited Central Park in New York, and they were in front of the United Nations. We had some good conversations there.

Often my family traveled with me and the birds. That's another thing that I particularly liked about this project -- how intertwined my personal life, with my kids and my husband, was all jumbled up together with this art project. I just liked that.

This circle was in the middle of a Thanksgiving celebration the birds were invited to be part of.

This was in front of Chartres Cathedral -- something we were just talking about one day, "wouldn't it be cool to have them

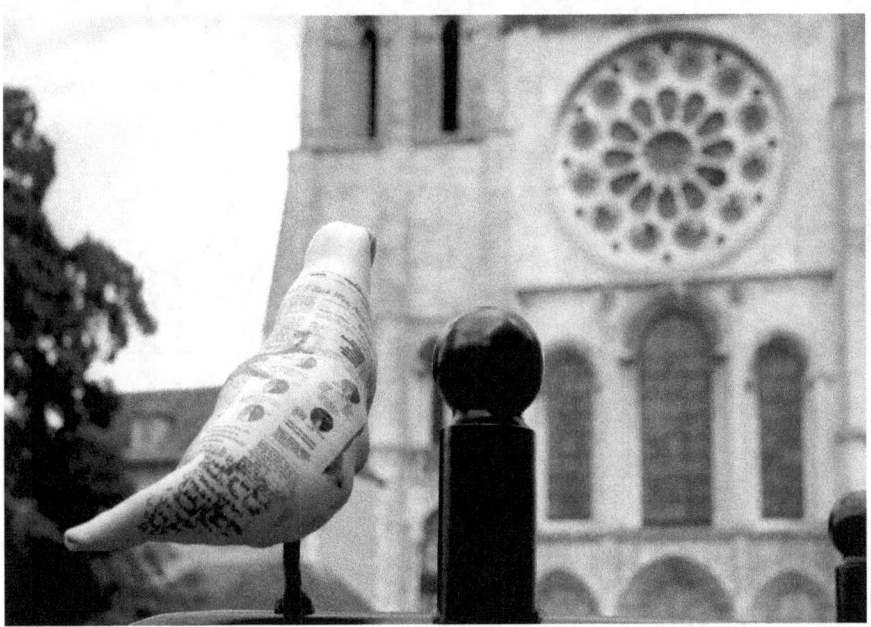

Birds In The Park

there," so we arranged finally to get permission to bring them there. My husband's from Germany, so a lot of the places that the birds landed, were kind of along our pathways of friends we could stay with.

I did not get any major grant for this. We did it all on a shoestring budget. We took the birds as checked luggage in 4 Samsonite suitcases when we flew. When we drove, we could bring more. This is in Germany, and I got to meet the real Bird Lady. People started to call me the Bird Lady, but then I met this person. She arrived to feed the birds, and she saw my birds -- and she's kind of got bad eyesight, and she thought that she had a whole new flock that she was going to have to take care of. [laughter]

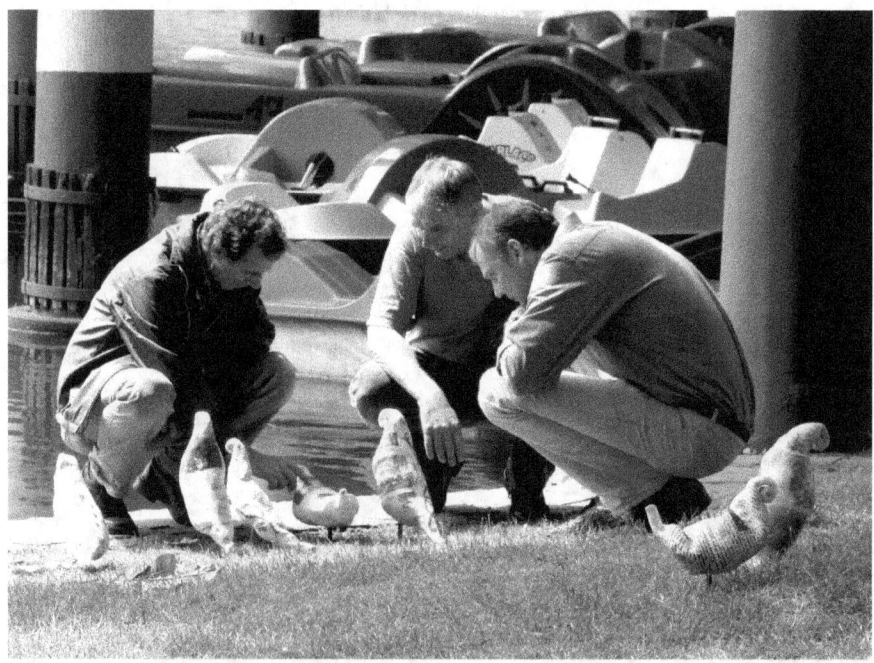

Birds In The Park

The farthest-away place that the birds went was the Galapagos Islands. In a way there it became a little something different. It was almost like a side line, where there was this whole thing about the interaction with animals, and just the curiosity of the animals with the birds, and of course the fun photographs. It was obviously not as much about being with people. Also, our friend who we were with on the Galapagos

Islands had an underwater camera, so he took these photos.

One of the most meaningful stops for the birds, for me... it's funny -- early on, I was feeling a little uncomfortable because I wanted to talk about my experience as a U.S. citizen, in regards to the war and wars that were being started kind of in my, our, name. Meanwhile, of course I did not have personal experience of war, the way that so many people do. So in some ways I felt a little bit like a charlatan to even be talking about it. What do I know? The funny thing is, two thirds into the project, I realized that I had some personal history that was very important in regards to this.

My father's father was an optical scientist in Germany -- my father's from Germany -- and basically, during World War II, my grandfather was working on the V1 and V2 missiles. Basically, building bombs for Hitler. It's something that I knew about in my family history, although I knew more about the more glory story later on; those same scientists went on to Cape Canaveral to be part of the whole space, man-on-the-moon projects -- the space program with NASA.

The earlier work is really in my mind, problematic. I have thought a lot about the work that people do in the world, and sometimes it's very difficult, the situations that people find themselves in. I hope that I have been able to not see things as black and white, and be too judgmental one way or another, but in fact this kind of art project is also a way for me to explore all these feelings about it.

There's a place called Peenemünde in Germany, which is

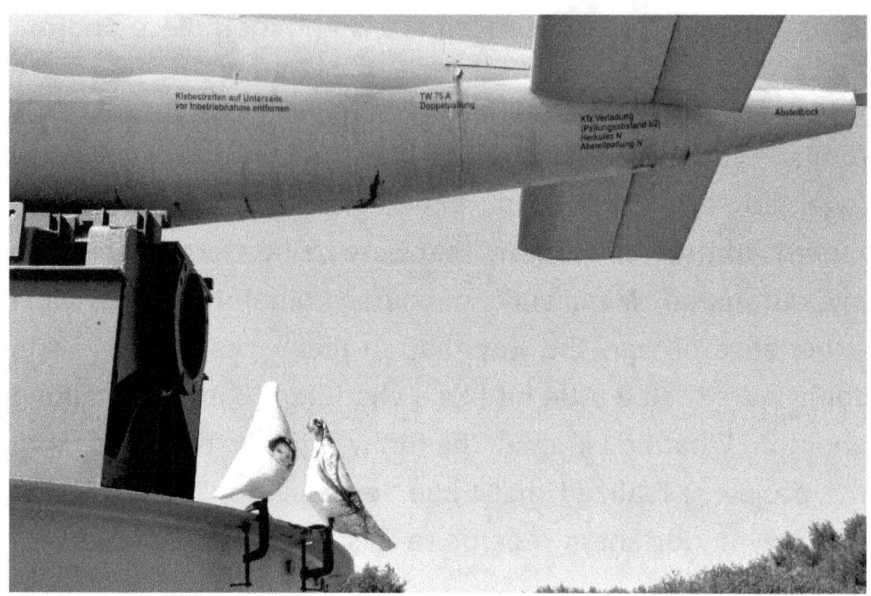

Birds In The Park

where the V1 and V2 rockets were built. My dad was a child there during World War II. Actually at a certain point, his house was completely bombed, and then he didn't live there anymore. We found out that a museum had just been built there on that spot in Peenemünde, and that the museum had started to act as a peace conference location, in some regards, in addition to being a museum that looked at this whole history -- this very specific history of building the V1 and V2 rockets. We found out about the museum, and I wrote to them and told them about this bird project, and also who my grandfather was, and that my dad had been a child there, and they invited the birds to come land there. They also invited my father to come, to give a talk about what he remembered of his experiences there.

So we went all, as a family. Me, my husband Helmut, the kids Oliver and Eliza, my mom and dad, and also a film crew, that by now was starting to make a documentary film about this project, and it definitely felt like something coming full circle. When the birds were there, and having conversations with people, not actually resolving things, but for me it felt really healthy to do that.

I started to make birds for some of the places specifically, so some of the birds that landed at Peenemünde had images of the stuff there; the scientist quarters, from old photographs my dad had given, plus some writing he had done about when his house was bombed, and about that time, about those questions.

After traveling for three or four years with the birds, I did what I considered to be the 'Last Landing' at the Railyard Park, here in Santa Fe, kind of bringing it all home. It was very early in the morning, setting up. It was really great to wrap it up that way in my own community.

I didn't actually wrap it up. It turns out the birds have had several lives. I'm not going to talk about the other parts of this project, except that it's been a really great vehicle. One of the things that I've loved about doing it, is that it involves both the creation of objects -- I just really love making things, and working with actual physical materials to create an art object -- and that it has this other aspect of something that goes beyond the object, and that involves relationships with people, which of course is much more intangible.

And I think that is it. [applause]

Audience Member:

I just wanted to clarify. So you would set them up very early morning, and would just leave them for a day, and then remove them that night?

Christy Hengst:

Yes, it was about four hours of setting up and taking down, for eight hours of them being there. It's crazy!

Audience Member:

Could you address why you used the bird form for that.

Christy Hengst:

First of all it was an accident. They just started to look like birds. But then, obviously, there's so much symbolic meaning in the bird, and so, around peace; I was looking at war and peace. And then, the way that they were moving around. Every time I did an installation it was called a Landing, and they really flew, all around, from place to place, and I was their wings.

Audience Member:

This is just a practical question. I know they were there, unprotected, and I just wondered: They were just such lovely things you can just take out of the ground and walk away with, I wonder if you ever lost any of them.

Christy Hengst:

Mainly I lost them in transit, in the suitcases. A few times I opened the suitcase and it was, Hmm, one, two, or three broken -- which was a bummer. There was only one time, it was across from the U.N. and there were some kids playing soccer, and they kicked it, but I don't think it was intentional. No, actually, nobody stole any, nobody intentionally hurt them, which is really nice. That was another thing that I just kind of intuitively liked, was placing these fragile things out in public, and sometimes, in the middle of a city. Just that kind of paradox.

Audience Member:

There's a great film about it, you can get the DVD from Christy. There's also a book, Axle published, which you can get from Axle, or Christy.

Christy Hengst:

I just wanted to say a couple of things before we all go.

One is, thank you so much, every person, for being here. I really appreciate it. Thank you to CCA, for hosting this. It's really great. They're not charging rent for us to do this. It's a community offering, and so if anybody wants to give a donation, that would be much appreciated. I think it's over there by the entrance.

Also thank you to Axle. This is part of the Economologies series that they've been doing, and they're just so great, all the different things that they produce. As a matter of fact, I think that when you leave, the truck is going to be open if anyone wants to come and peek in at the exhibit that's there right now.

We are going to meet back here shortly before 3pm, and I hope that all of you come back, it's going to be a completely different thing. It's a panel discussion, a roundtable -- or a rectangular table -- that is going to be moderated by Michelle Laflamme-Childs. She has prepared questions for specific people, and that's the first part of it, and then we actually want to hear your thoughts on those questions and others afterwards.

Thanks!

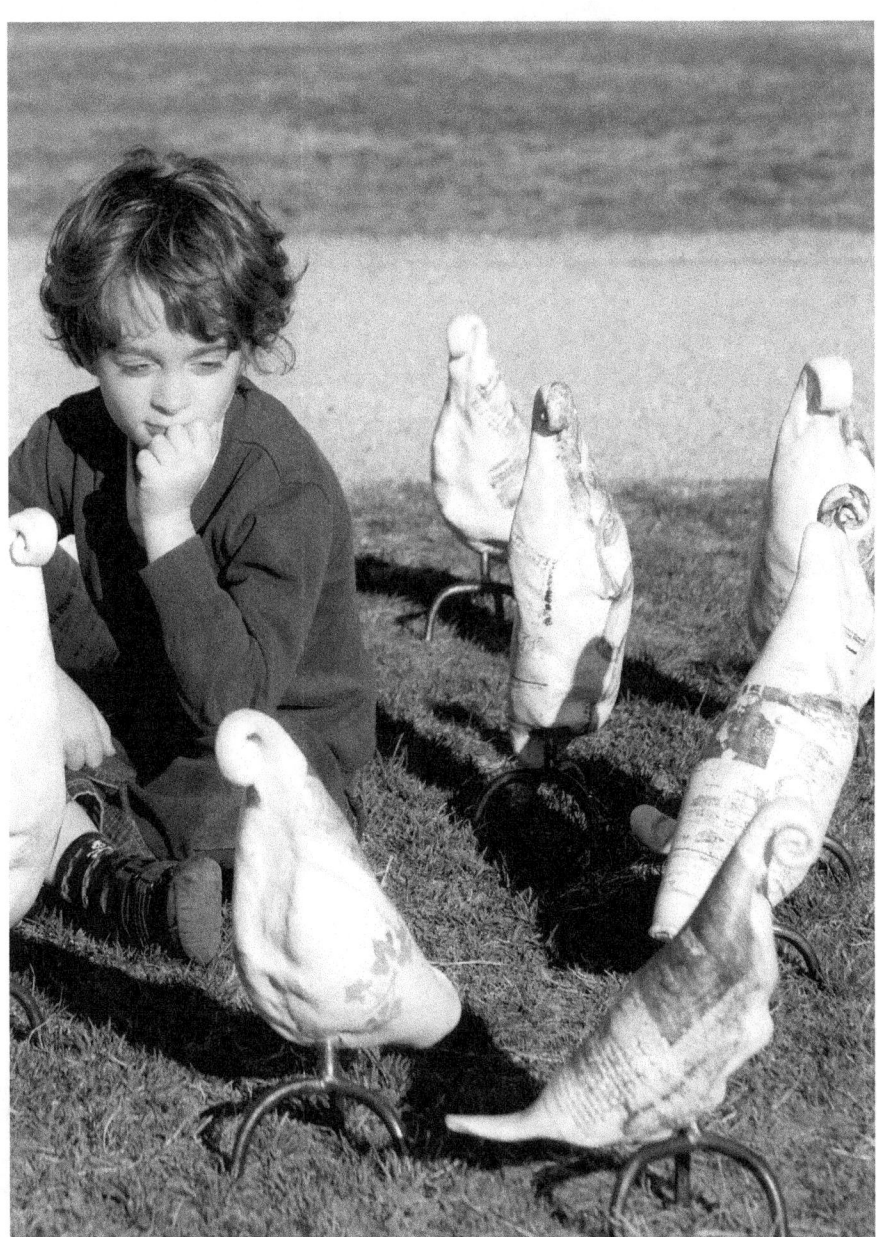

Birds In The Park

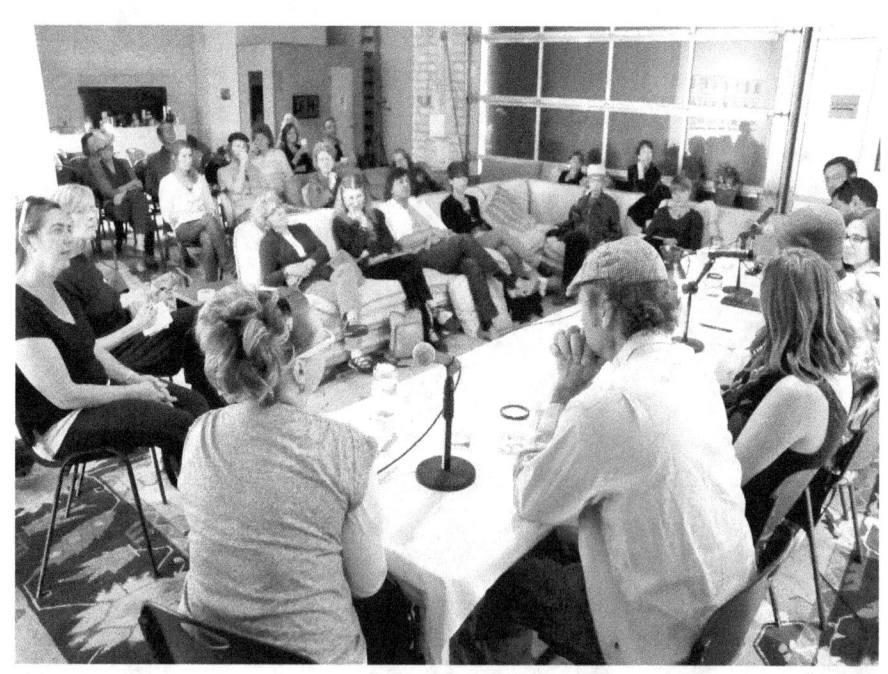

146

ROUNDTABLE DISCUSSION

Moderated by
Michelle Laflamme-Childs

Paula Castillo

Vince Kadlubek

Issa Nyaphaga

Sanjit Sethi

Alysha Shaw

Jerry Wellman

Michelle Laflamme-Childs:

Thank you, Christy, for doing this. Was it a year ago that we saw each other at Collected Works, and you were like, "I'm thinking about this thing," and then all of a sudden it's here. Congratulations, that's amazing.

So for each of you, this is going to be in 60 seconds or less. Can you condense your whole life, and let us know.... why you do what you do, and what you do -- probably in the opposite order than I said it? [laughter]

Jerry Wellman:

I'll take this -- 60 seconds? -- hmmm, well, I'm an artist, and I've done a lot of different exploration into that territory, so it has shifted and changed over the years. Most recently, most of my energy has gone into the creation of Axle

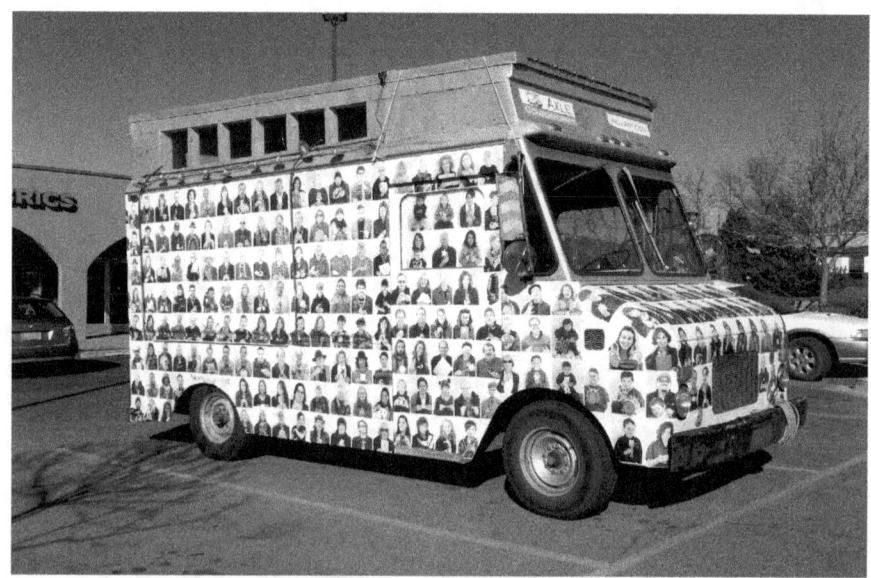

Axle Contemporary

Contemporary. Looking over the audience, I think almost everybody knows what that is. I've always been interested in widening the definitions of what art is, and could be, and basically, community and communication. That's where this has landed me..... in 60 seconds. [laughter]

Christy Hengst:

How about a little more than 60 seconds? Say something about what kind of artwork you have done yourself.

Michelle Laflamme-Childs:

Yes, please. Your personal practice.

Jerry Wellman:

My personal practice? Gosh. I've done performance art, and I've done video work. I started doing painting, but they're so cumbersome and big, so I didn't like the painting at a point, and I kept reducing that, and I really like the digital situation. Now I've got something that's 6 foot by 10 foot by [laughs] 9 foot or whatever. Much bigger, but it is pretty mobile.

I've been pretty influenced by the teachings of Joseph Beuys, which some of you may know who he is, or you may not. Not so much his artwork, but where he's coming from as a person, which is in many ways trying to combine mystic or spiritual values, and poetic values.

They would say that he's one of the big conceptual artists, but his work is much juicier in my mind than many conceptual artists' work, and most especially his teaching.

If there was more time I would talk more about him.   Equally important to me, is Art Brut, the art of the insane.

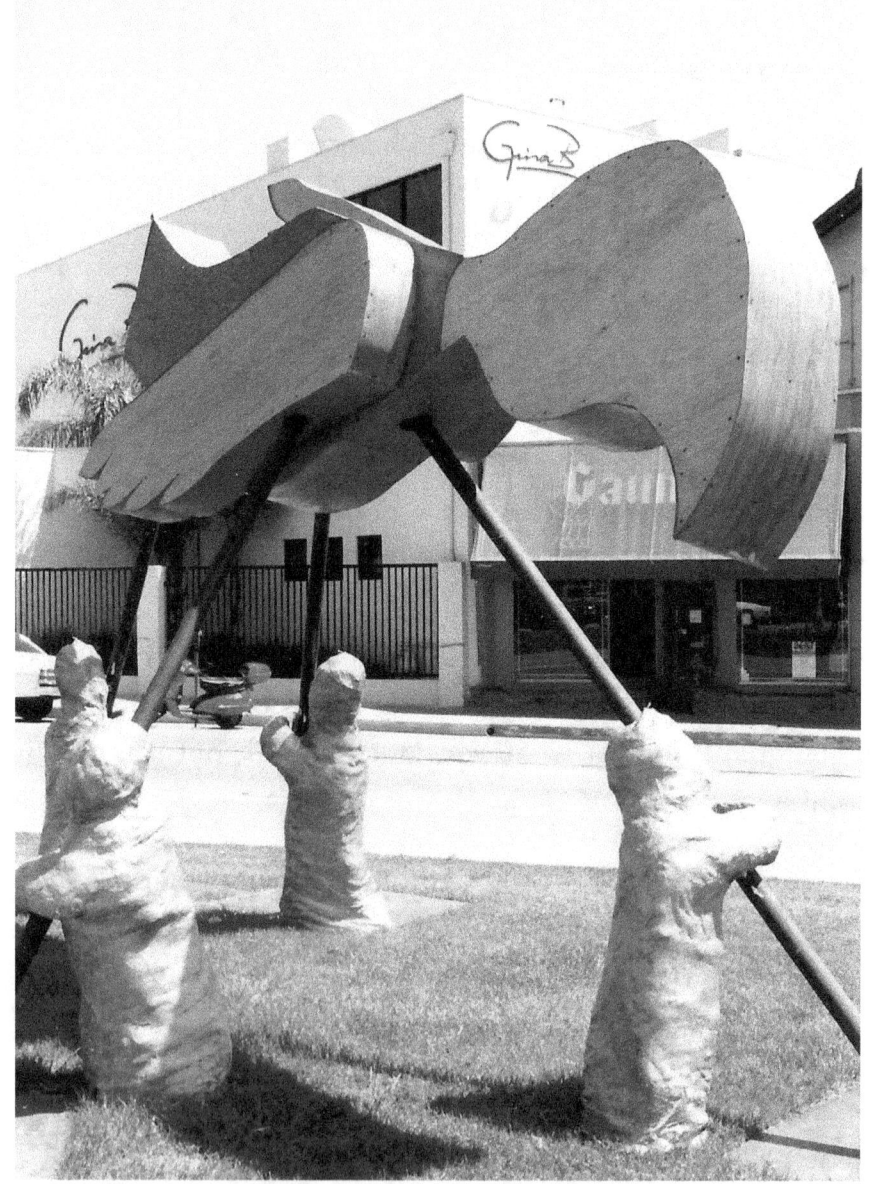

Jerry Wellman *Peripatetic Phantom of the Clouds*

Alysha Shaw:

II'm Alysha Shaw, and I'm an interdisciplinary artist, and a community organizer. I've long been trying to figure out how to live in that intersection -- how to function politically as an artist, and how to function artistically as a political person -- and where does that lie? I'm really interested in the social impact of art.

I coordinate the Lifesongs program. I work with Molly Sturges and Acushla Bastible on that, and with Aly at the Academy. Personally, I've just explored myself as a political person, by doing interventions like tarot card readings at the legislature, Really interesting cards come up on those people. [laughter]

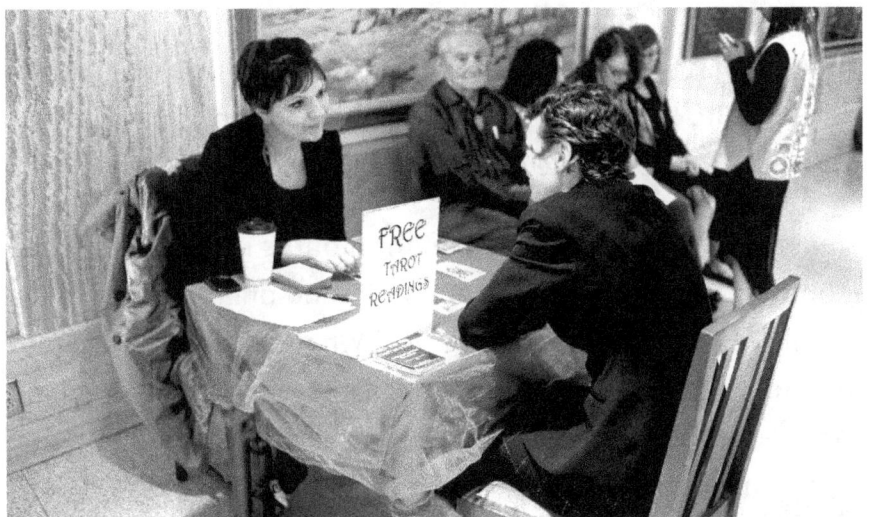

Alysha Shaw *Tarot Card Reading*

There's a newspaper back there I recently made. It highlights the stories, voices, and experiences of people in Santa Fe that I think go under the radar, that aren't included in our dominant narrative. I'm a musician as well. I'm interested in public art as a kind of "neo-folk" practice.

In a way, I think that social practice as it manifests, tends to kind of fill in the hole that capitalist society has left in all of us. To take art out of the commercial and the individual, and make it something that we all can share, and build communities. I'm really excited for this conversation.

Issa Nyaphaga:

Hi, my name is Issa Nyaphaga. I am a visual artist, and a social justice activist. Lately I've been starting a community radio for one million people in Cameroon. Those people cannot access their own information, and they can't make a phone call...they need help.

That's my latest project. But I am also running an organization called HITIP, Hope International for Tikar People. Because my tribe lives in the middle of the Equatorial Forest in Cameroon.

What I do in the West, I spend eight months in Santa Fe. Three months in Cameroon in the summer, and one month with my son in Paris where I used to live. What people know about my story, that I came from a resilient process, after being tortured in prison because I was a political cartoonist. One of the things that I'm very proud of, is that I kept making art, because I was an artist. I healed myself through art, and I forgive everybody who have done that. So I'm returning to the same country to make change. This is based on the power that I extract from art, and art ideas, to activate. This is my story. Thank you. I'm very happy to be here.

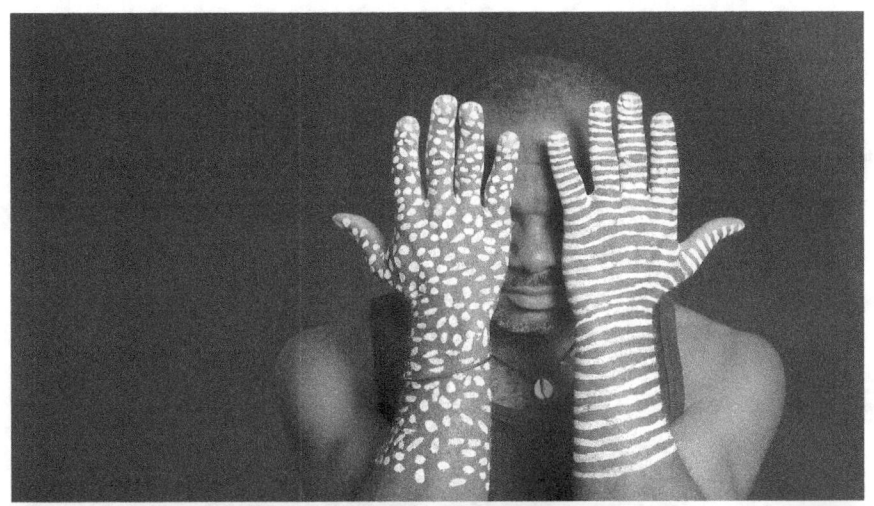

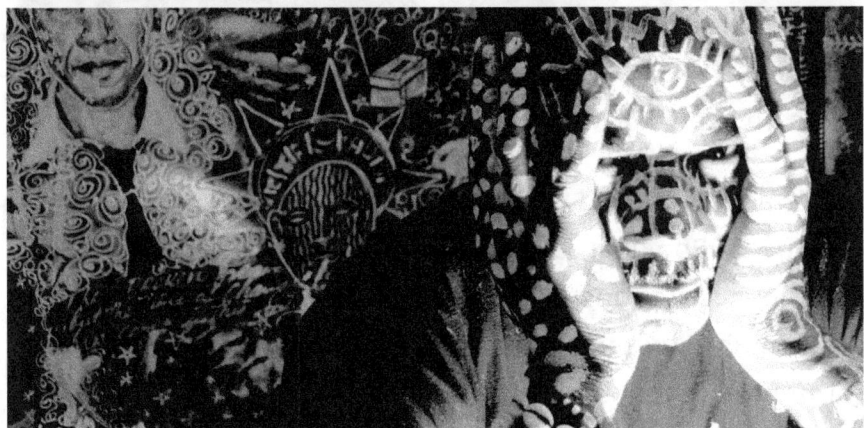

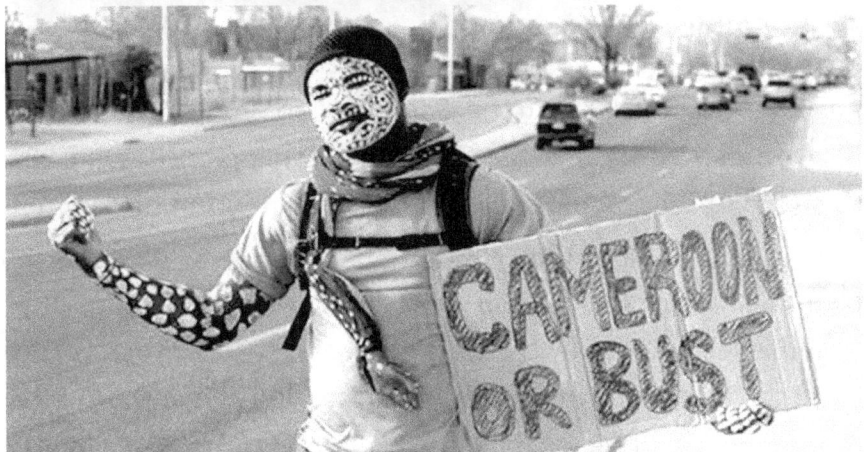

Issa Nyaphaga *Urban Way*

Paula Castillo:

I'm Paula Castillo. I'm a native New Mexican, I live up in Cordova, which is a little community between Chimayo and Truchas. Most people know me as a metal sculptor. But I kind of see myself as a spy, someone who is interested in the abyss. One of the things I'm very interested in, in New Mexico, is the lack of access of rural people, and their voices, in the state.

I'm also very interested in the environment. I've done a lot of very large scale, as Edie called it, "shiny" projects, which I'm very proud of, as well as creating objects for art galleries in Santa Fe especially.

Years ago, I started an anonymous practice that's inspired by Murray Bookchin and Anarchist Thought. I have done a lot of collaborations, secret collaborations that don't require any funding, but are very satisfying, and I hope satisfying for former audiences who are the participants in it.

Sanjit Sethi:

I'm Sanjit Sethi, E.D. at the Santa Fe Art Institute. When I have the spare time, I also have my own practice, which at this stage predominantly focuses on the creation of counter-monuments and counter-memorials, looking at histories of trauma that exist on a personal level, or on a community-based level, or on a socio-ethnic level, and seeing projects that can act without any of the baggage that you see in traditional monuments and memorials. So, it's a memorial that's smell-based... or one that's explicitly temporal in nature. Those

154

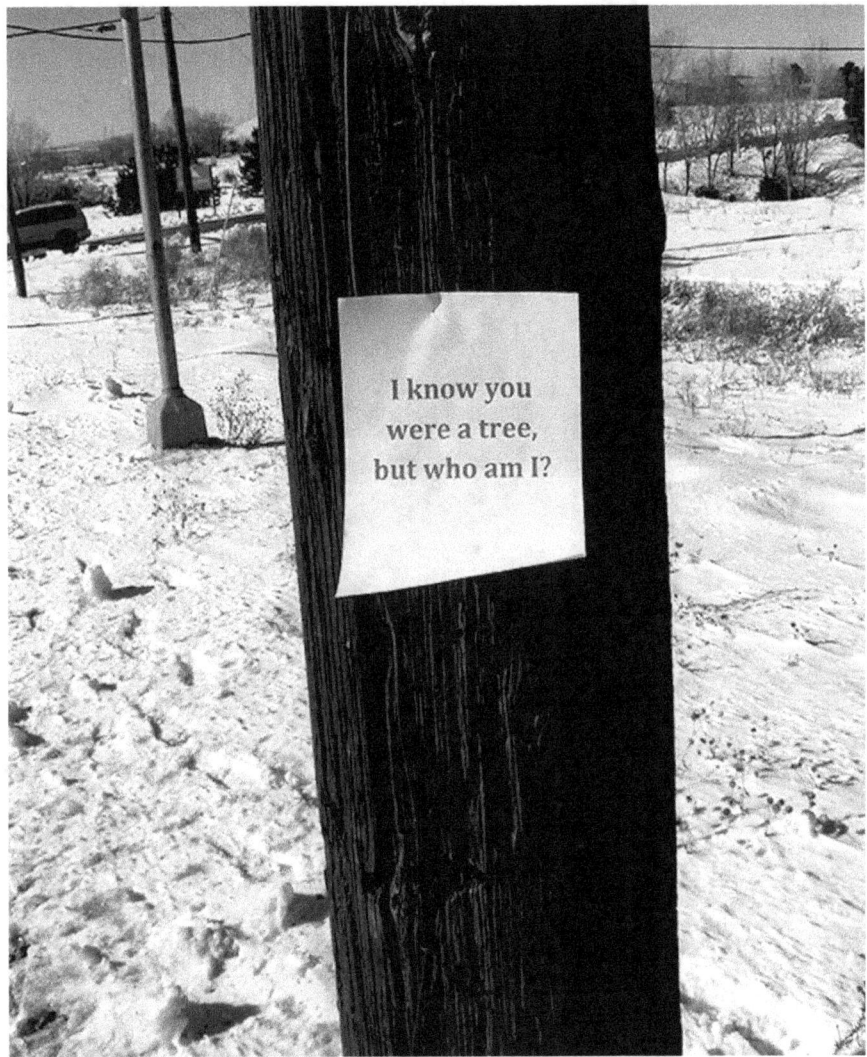

Paula Castillo *Love Letters to Trees*

are some of the areas of interest. The way that I think I'm able to converge ideas within my own practice, and the incredible productive and rewarding day job that I have, is really through the territory around critical inquiry.

I really like questions. I like well-formed questions. I like thoughtful questions. And I like to go ahead and push dialogues forward by examining: What are the premises and some of those initial thoughts that we have, and how do we go ahead and shape this as a dialogue? I think in doing so, it's focused, again, on that territory around critical inquiry.

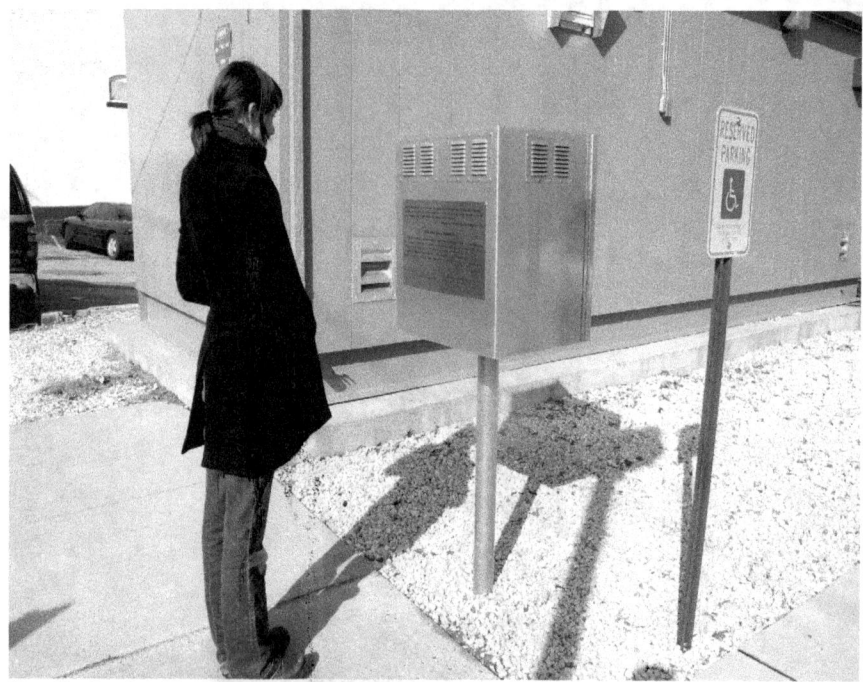

Sanjit Sethi *Kumi Wada Bakery Rememberance*

Vince Kadlubek:

I'm Vince Kadlubek. I'm here representing a group, a production company, called Meow Wolf. Basically, Meow Wolf is an open door collaborative that does whatever cultural events it feels like doing. I end up representing Meow Wolf a lot because I'm the one who's always wanting to do stuff. Anybody could do anything, and we don't really have any rules to it. It's kind of a shit show, it's also really

156

beautiful at the same time.

Personally, the role that I play with that group is very much like the organizer of people, organizer of artists, thinking more on the business side of things, or proposals, grants, stuff like that. As an individual, I post a lot on Facebook. That's my main social practice, social arts practice, is posting status updates and trying to get as many likes as I can, as many shares as I can. [laughter]

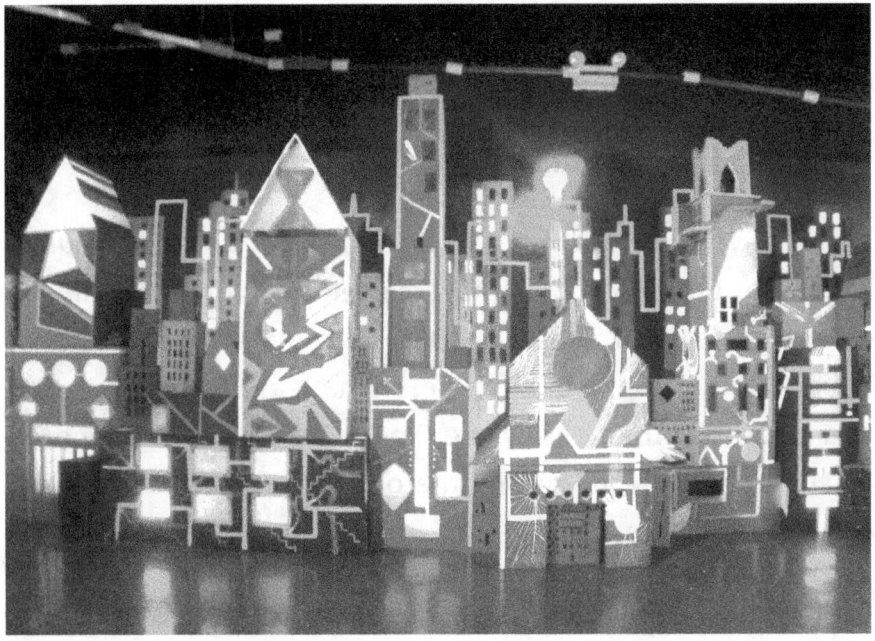

Meow Wolf *Glitteropolis*

I'm pretty convinced that I'm going to be able to cash in my likes at some point [laughter] because I'm broke. It would be really nice if I can. But I also do a lot of individual projects. I started a project called "Santa Fe Stories Project," which was very much inspired by Edie and the Snow Poems, which is the idea that you have site-specific experiences of information that pop up around town. Mine, though, are based on Santa Fe's history.

I'm interested in the history of Santa Fe, the post-World War II history, from 1950 to 1990 or 95 -- basically when we went from a small town to an international city, that period of transition. I'm really interested in capturing how Santa Fe was before we became an international tourist destination. I'm in the midst of working on that project. I'm really big on Galaga, and I have a public art project that's about to launch, based on that video game from the '80s, called Galaga. That's called The Adventures of Galaga Lubek. That's it.

Michelle Laflamme-Childs:

Those of you who know me know that I'm not afraid of public speaking, typically. But I have to tell you that, that sitting at the table with these people, I am incredibly nervous. [laughter] If I fumble or stumble, then please forgive me. But you just heard them. Holy cat. This is amazing. I'm honored to sit here with you, and be the one tasked with asking you questions.

Christy and I talked in advance a little bit about how to format this, to make sure that we touched on a couple of different things, but also that everyone had a chance to speak. Because sometimes.. you've probably been to panel discussions where one person just goes on forever and nobody intervenes. I figured we have approximately 10 minutes apiece, because we have about an hour to talk, and I have a question or series of questions, for each of you. Some of them are based on questions that we threw around in email in advance, so they're not unfamiliar probably. Some of them aren't. But there's nothing too crazy. I'm just going to start with Alysha, because her name starts with A. [laughter]

Alysha, Your political work clearly has heavy influence in your personal work, your personal artistic practice. When we were bandying all these questions around, you gave us a long list of questions that you had developed in an exercise in a workshop with Paul Ramirez Jonas, and a couple of them really stuck with me.

I thought it was an incredible procedure -- the way that they did it was to write down a hundred questions on index cards without thinking too much about what they are, on the topic on which they were trying to ruminate. Alysha sent us a few of those.

One of them that I think is really interesting, particularly in relationship to your political involvement is... here's the question as you wrote it: "Is 'participation' as problematic in art as it is in politics?"

Because you wrote participation in quotes, I would love it if you would talk about what you mean by participation, first of all. Then, because really so much of our conversation right now, about public art, centers on the ideas of audience, viewer, participant, community, experience -- and less on the art object, I wanted you to talk a little bit about participation and then answer your own question about the problematic nature of it, with regard to art and politics.

Alysha Shaw:

All right. [laughter] I was actually kind of afraid that one of those questions would come back to bite me.

Well, I think 'participation' has kind of become this buzzword, right, in this type of art. There are many different levels of engagement that we have in life, and socially engaged art, and certainly in politics. I worked on a number of political campaigns, in New Mexico. They totally burned me out, and they totally disillusioned me with the process. I'm still recovering from that all. I'd say that that type of participation, to me, that comes in that form, that political campaign form, is very disingenuous. It's very much about, "How can I use you? How can I turn you out to vote? How can I woo you with three glossy talking points and a spectacularized image of someone with a great smile?"

It really reduces complex issues in communities to simplified things that divide people, in my estimation. This is by no means absolute. This is just my thought on it. That's how I view participation in politics. I think, when you get to real grassroots community organizing, you see someone who creates a space, that... actually I have a specific example.

We were talking about this at lunch. In 2009, I worked at a community center in the Hopewell/Mann neighborhood, in the center of the city. I could give you statistics, but it's got a third of the city's entire affordable housing rental stock, a huge immigrant community and a lot of fear, a lot of poverty, and also a lot of beautiful culture.

We created a community center. A woman, Soledad Santiago, led this effort. She created this amazing space where she just invited people in. It became a space for quinceañeras. It became a space for potlucks. It became a space where kids would come and play video games on the computers after school. It became a space where we made a garden together.

The community actually owned that space and directed what we did with it. They organized a food distribution service, through the Food Depot. They created a women's collective that made these beautiful artworks and sold them. That, to me, is exemplary of... I wouldn't even call it participation. I think 'participation' is problematic, because it implies this static relationship, where you're the participant and you're engaging with me in this way that I define for you. Rather, these folks became invited into a space, and they defined it. They became collaborators, and they drove the vision.

For me, that's analogous to the kind of socially engaged art that I like and want to be a part of. I think it's very easy to go into a neighborhood, or to work with a community and public, and have your ideas about how you're going to engage with them, and how the participants are going to engage.

In some cases, it can be so off that you don't even have any participants. I find that word, 'participation,' problematic. I would honestly prefer not to use it, because of what it implies for me.

I think that the most beautiful... not the most beautiful, because I think that, when you have socially engaged projects,

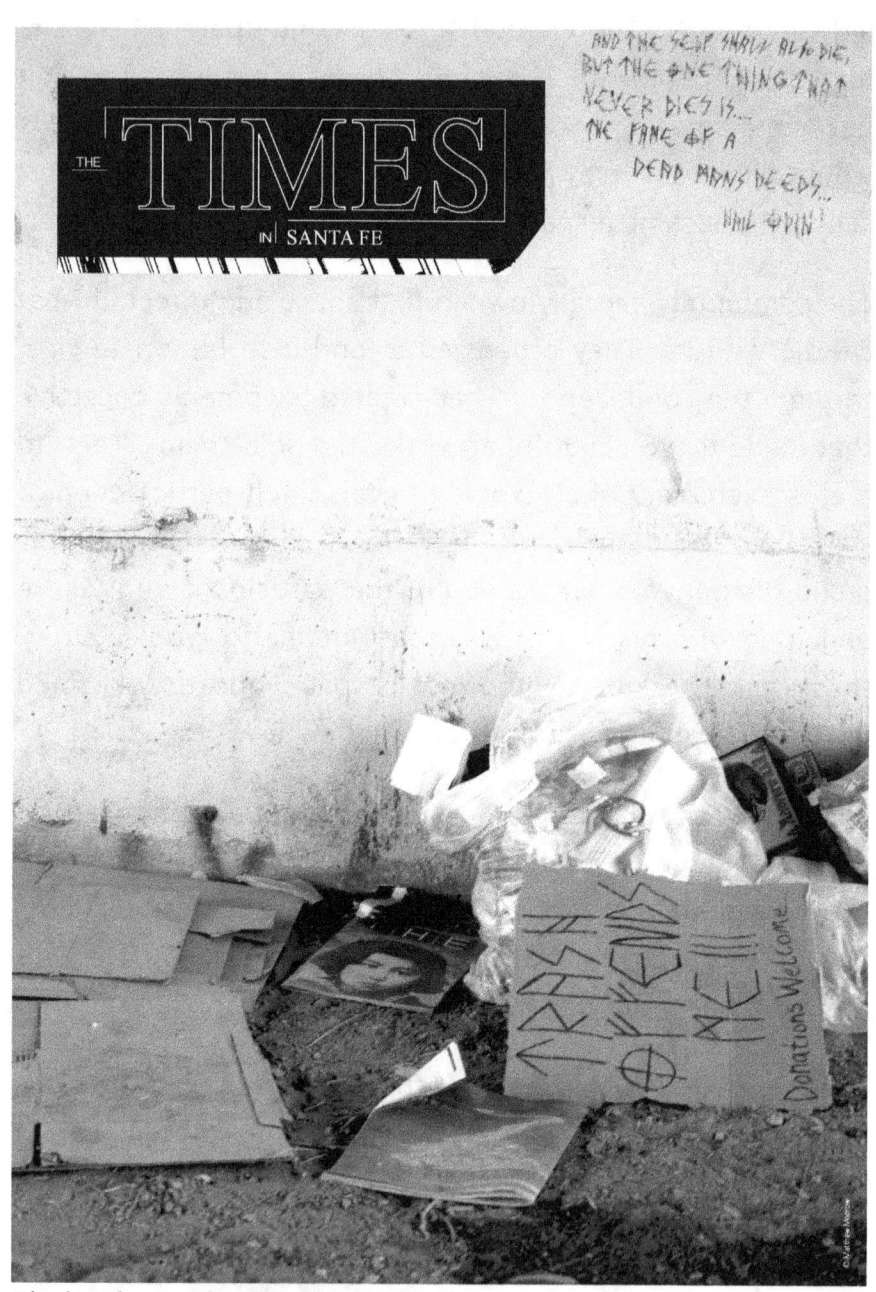

Alysha Shaw *The Times in Santa Fe*

you've got different levels of engagement and they're relative to the intention of the artist. But, for those really multilayered, long-term projects -- I can use Lifesongs and El Otro Lado for example.

Aly and I are not the founders of the programs that we work on, by any means, but we're becoming empowered, in a way, to facilitate them, to help them grow, to build them. I think that's a beautiful model, where you can start something in the community and then you can empower others to make it live beyond you, and you can walk away, as an artist. I hope that answers the question.

Michelle Laflamme-Childs:

Does anyone want to address any of that at all? If not, that leads me nicely into my question for Vince.

Vince Kadlubek:

Okay. I was thinking about how to respond to that...

Michelle Laflamme-Childs:

Perfect, because Alysha talked about participation being a problematic term. You, Vince, when we were throwing all of our questions around, came back with: Does the language that we use in talking about social engaged art and community engagement and all of the language that we as artists and administrators, wrap around what we're talking about? Does that very language alienate the people we're looking to engage or participate?

When you first wrote that, I was like, "Well, that's obnoxious." But after stewing on it, I thought, "That's really a reasonable and important question that needs to be asked." Since you're the one that threw it out there, I thought maybe you might want to address it.

Vince Kadlubek:

Expand on that, yeah. Watching Matthew's presentation about the Gourdsign project, it's really awesome because there was no approval process. You didn't need to put it into a language for anybody, and there was a purity to it. You also didn't have any money for it, so there was a lack of funding for it.

The majority of times that we're talking about social engagement with our art, or public art, or social practice through art, we're seeking funding. The funding comes from a different audience than the demographic we're trying to reach. There are different languages there.

We have to form our language based on, to be honest, rich white people, and the language that rich white people speak. When the majority of the time we're trying to reach non-rich, non-white people. As an organization, you have the ability to get lost in those whimsical sentences, and those paragraphs that sound so good to a granting organization. [laughter]

You start to become not only defined by it, but you surround yourself by it. Because, the language we use creates the community that we are engaged with. If we use that language, we end up surrounding ourselves with all those who also use that language.

I think we're all in this room together, right now, because we all use that language. Thus, the community in this room right now is based on the language of the flyer that was made, or the name of the event. How many people can hear the name of the event, that don't understand this language, and say, "That's something I want to go to and learn about?"

Recognizing that when we talk about reaching out to the public, in whatever form, that the public is so much larger than what the art world is. The art world is five, ten percent of the public.

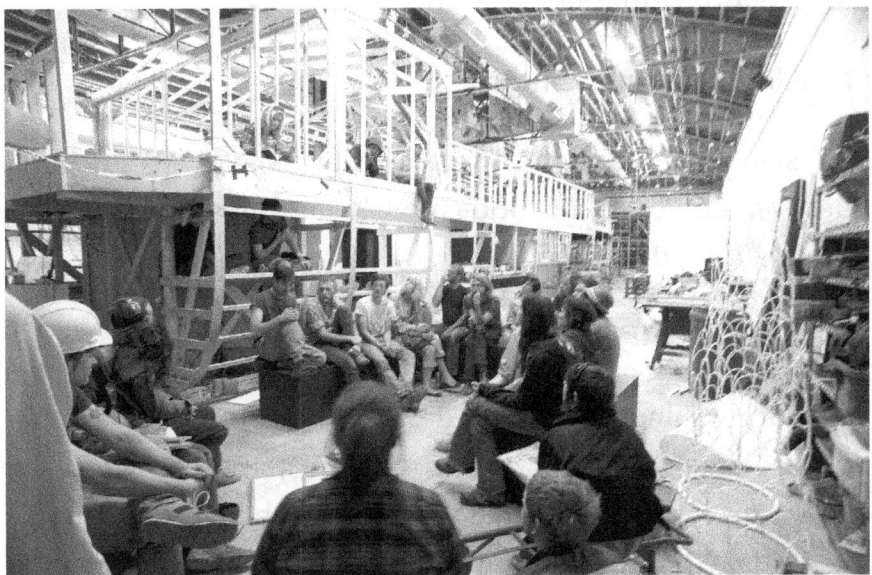

Meow Wolf *The Due Return*

So many of our issues -- like listening to Molly talk about climate change, "This is a terrible project for an artist to try to tackle." Ultimately, it's because 80 percent of the people don't vote. 40 percent of the people who still do vote don't understand the effect of climate change.

We're talking about 90 percent of the population that we need to reach with our public art, or public campaign about climate change -- 90 percent of those people don't really even get it.

We're speaking a language that... we're preaching to the choir. We're speaking language for that 10 percent. I don't know the solution, other than really monitoring the words that we use, actual words that we write down, the actual words that come out of our mouths. Simplifying, and getting the college educated lawyer talk and foundation talk, and trying our best to reject it.

Michelle Laflamme-Childs:

You said you didn't have an answer. That was my next question, do you have suggestions? But I guess that's it, to be mindful of that.

Vince Kadlubek:

Some other things, too. I sat down with Chrissie at the Tune-up Cafe and we talked about this. We talked about social engagement, and engagement with the public through art. A lot of times, organizations... I got in trouble for naming organizations in the past, and I won't. But a lot of times organizations build their building, plant their flag, and say, "Okay. We're open to the public. We are open for public engagement." That's not public engagement. That's you hoping that the public will engage with you. That's you hoping that they take on the role of public engagement. You as an organization, you've got to go to Nava and Gonzales and Turquoise Trail. You have to go in to those communities. You have to go to Hopewell.

You can't sit back and say, "Where are they? We put flyers out." If you want to be known as an arts organization that is doing public work, then you have to be in those communities. Santa Fe has a few examples, and I think across the country a lot of organizations sort of rest on their laurels. It's about getting funding based on this narrative that you've created, and not actually making any difference.

Then the money gets lost in administrative costs, and you have an organization that's got a $200,000 operating budget, and 80 of it is going to one person, who needs to pay off a mortgage. He or she can't change their salary, because they have a mortgage to pay off, and they're struggling artists just like everybody else. Nobody wants to call them out for it, because the art world is so nice. If you say something nasty, somebody stands up and yells at you, at a panel discussion. [laughter]

You know? People have to be called out on this stuff. If you claim to be an organization that's trying to help and to have an outreach, then you have to outreach.

Michelle Laflamme-Childs:

I was recently in Artesia, New Mexico -- prior to hearing about all of the immigration issues -- for an arts and cultural district. They just were named a State Arts and Cultural District.

One of the things that came up was: Why weren't more of the Latino population participating in the events that they were having at these venues. We asked, "What are you doing?" and they said, "We had a mariachi band come." [laughter]

It's absolutely about that, what they think they need to do to bring in a community, instead of going to the community. Your example with the project...

Vince Kadlubek:

Or with the Love of Learning project.

Michelle Laflamme-Childs: Going to the kids in the schools, or going to these communities, or with the community center project. I think that's critical.

Alysha Shaw:

How do we go into communities as outsiders, as organizations, as artists? Because, it's not that easy sometimes, you know? I don't know if that's something you want to respond to?

Vince Kadlubek:

I'm lucky enough, when we talk about, let's say, the Southside community, or lower-income, Hispanic community in Santa Fe, I've always felt protected, because I was born and raised here.

To me it comes back to language. There's a recognition of a language and you speak that language. If you can speak that language -- and it has to do with dialect, it has to do with a way of communicating -- you have to really check your language. You can't speak your speak in a community that doesn't speak your speak.

I've been able to adapt, at least in Santa Fe, to that. But I'd say that finding people, pinpointing people in the community.

I'm sure you guys probably did this on Hopewell. There were probably people who stepped us as leaders from within -- You pinpoint them, and you empower them.

It's scary. It goes back to what you were saying, Alysha. It's scary, because you have to let go of your organization, and let go of your vision, because you're handing it off to a more, in some ways, authentic leader from that community that you're trying to reach. You have to let go of what you think, and let them run with it some. I think that's an important thing.

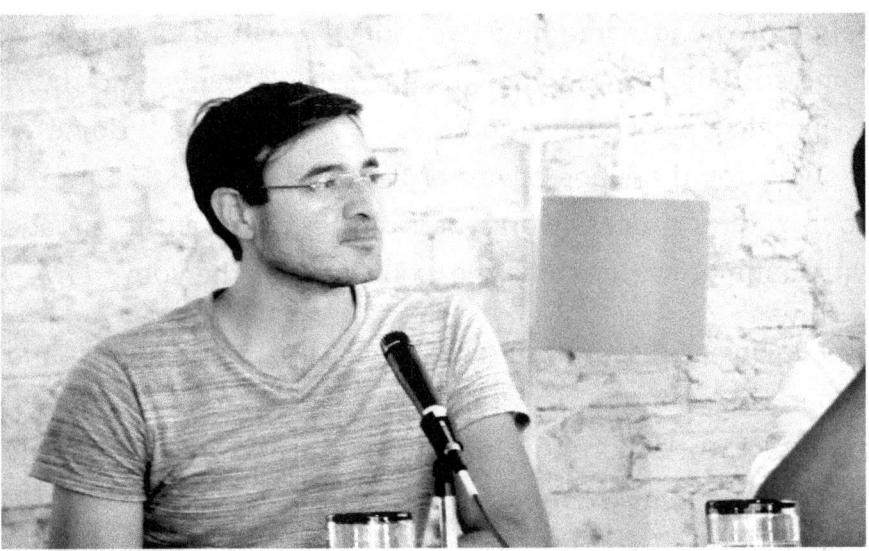

Vince Kadlubek

Issa Nyaphaga:

Well, I'd like to share a story... it varies. When I lived in Paris, I used to be a community leader and educator, so I would engage the community population to make art out of recycling. The reason why the City Hall called me to do that is because, in that neighborhood, people eat pizza or drink water and just trash the bottle out the window.

So they called me to do that. The first project I did with them was to make art in some sort of studio with the neighbors, people who show up. Then, we put the sculpture outside, in the neighborhood, and somebody passed by and burned it.

So, we rethought the way we could do that project, in that neighborhood, and decided to set up the studio outside.

Everybody can paint outside. If you actually see your neighbor doing something, art out of trash or engaging in some social project in your neighborhood, you will not burn it. Because it's your neighbor, and you saw them doing it, and you could engage or not engage, up to you. I think the door-by-door process works better when you want to engage with community. It works the same way for the vote.

I think we are disconnected from our tribal populations, and also in the West, (I always talk about the West and the South, because I work globally.) In the West, artists and politicians have become people very idealistic; they're the elite. To say, "I am an artist," you are not just anyone in the society. You are up there. When you talk to somebody who is struggling every day for a meal, or to get a job, you don't speak the same language. You speak something totally different. We have to rethink the way artists engage in society.

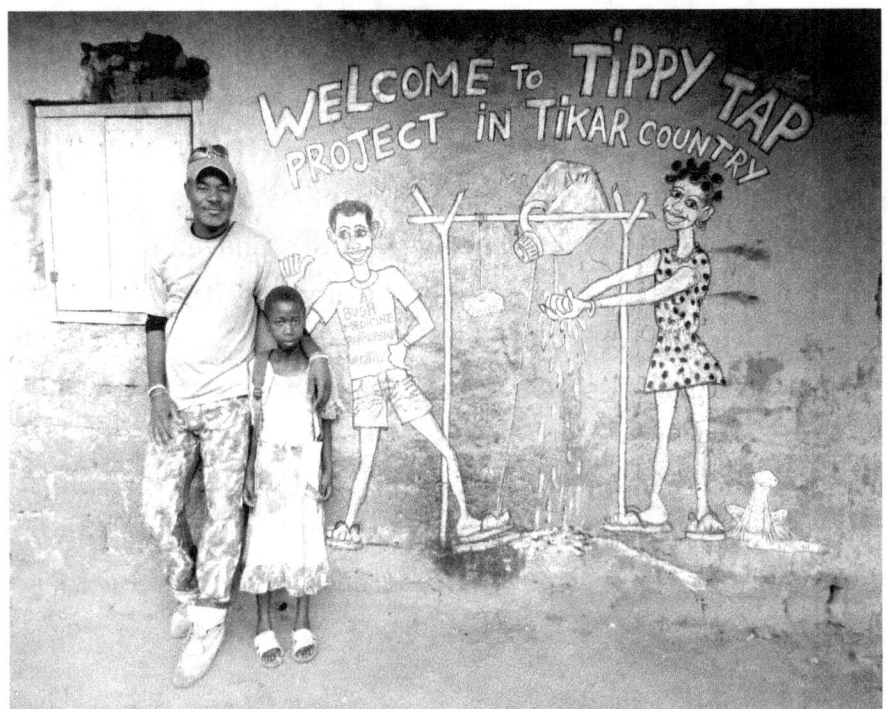

Issa Nyaphaga *Tippy Tapp*

Whether you're activists, or you're intellectuals and want to change society, you want to break your rules down, and go pick up trash anywhere, or go talk to any kind of person. Because I lived in France for 10 years, and before I came to the U.S., or went to China or Japan, I lived with people who came from all these parts of the world, so I could talk to them, and traveled this way.

So, I really don't see myself as a visual artist, I see myself as a people artist first, which can justify what I do today. We have to be connected, to be able to do that. That's my point.

Paula Castillo:

I understand what you are saying, the lack of access... It's definitely a crisis in communities, and our community here, locally. It reminds me of a story I once read about Cesar Chavez.

There was a journalist who came to follow him around, and he was an educated man from New York. Chavez noted that when he spoke to him, he spoke differently than when he spoke to his people, and it really irritated the shit out of him [laughs], because he thought that there was some kind of condescension in that. I think that we all come with masks, societal masks. In many ways, we are puppets, we really have no control over it. But I think that we have to be very careful with modifying Self to such a degree, that we create these false territories.

I see the solution in some of the, again, very anonymous projects that I've done, artists as, not hero, artist as very natural interloper, where you are creating a relationship with a person; they are creating a relationship with you. There is an equality in terms of compassion and empathy, recognition that we are all human. Not deficits, whatsoever, but connections. Making connections -- where do people have power and finding those spaces.

Michelle Laflamme-Childs:

Issa, what you said brings me, actually, to the questions that I had for you, nicely. Thank you for fitting right into my scheme here so beautifully. I wanted to ask you two separate questions, but with you, especially, you're such an integrated person to me, even though they are two separate questions, I'm sure they will be together in your mind in a way.

One was, I trying to separate -- and maybe that's the problem, is me trying to separate your artistic work from your non-profit activist work.

So I'm thinking about the Urban Way work that you do in particular, and that it is out there in public, that's a community thing. It's improvisational, public... you go to where people are, and people can come and participate in and witness this practice for you.

I was thinking about, (and I have a question similar to this for Paula as well), what you are thinking about when you are doing a piece like this, a performative piece, which is very personal to you, and a statement about your own issues with your home country, and the power that you now have, and/or lack, when it comes to them. When you are presenting something publicly, what are you thinking about with regards to what the public will take away from that, or what people who witness it will gain or learn from it? Is that part of it for you, or is it entirely really an internal thing?

Issa Nyaphaga:

[laughs] I thank you very much for that question. It's both. Maybe the public doesn't know this -- I body paint myself, with live music. The reason why I do this is because, about 21 years ago, I was tortured for two weeks by women who wanted to collect information from me. We were running

a newspaper for a non-literate population, and designed cartoons for them to be able to read and be informed.

My government created a censorship law to ban cartoons. We were a group of activists who thought that the law can be wrong. It's not because it's the law that it keeps people safe: Some laws can hurt people, we thought it was very wrong. We did not accept respecting the law.

So, some people paid with their lives, I only had to pay by being held for two weeks, hung by a woman from the ceiling. After that process, I went through therapy, and therapy wasn't enough for me. I was lucky that I got a gift from my mother to be an artist, and I found a way to start healing myself through art. That's what came out of that process, Urban Way.

When I do it, I heal myself in front of society, in the middle of people in public, with another musician -- but it's based on improvisation, because when I was in prison I listened to music a lot. Music really helped me to kill time, as we say it in French. I don't know if you say in English.

Music helped me a lot, and I read a lot of books. When I'm in that process, I also want to tell people to start their own process. Because the way I use Urban Way, it helps me to heal, and also helps me not to get revenge, not to get angry towards those people. So I forgave them a long time ago.

But because I lived my past life as an indigenous person, and now I'm living as a Westerner, life is duality. We have night and day, wrong and right, up and down, left and right.

Those are both part of me. I extract inspirational and artistic power from art in the West, and then go back to where I belong to, trying to reconnect. That's what I'm trying to do in my own life process.

But on my way, I'm trying to also positively give hope to people, because I came from where there is no running water, no electricity... After we had independence from French and British, 60 years ago, they told the population, "The reason why we are your leaders is because God chose us to rule you. You can't access education."

That's the moment when I came with my radio project and said, "That's crap. All of us can be educated." I think it's part of art. So, both processes are not divided, they are part of me, and they are me. They are the same thing.

Michelle Laflamme-Childs:

Do you see the projects like Radio Taboo Project, as art?

Issa Nyaphaga:

Yes. It's an art project... everybody can join the project. I'm grateful right now to have two filmmakers following me to tell the story. I'm also happy to have built the tower last year and put the radio up. I'm very fortunate for that.

Also, artists have something in art that's called the avant-garde. The avant-garde is a vision that somebody has, many years before it happens. You project your mind and think of people who could have: Internet, like 20 years ago or maybe

50 years ago, some people thought that today we may be using the internet, interfaces and chat with each other from China to the U.S. in seconds. Some people had that vision, they had an avant-garde vision.

Today, that's what I do with Radio Taboo. I think that people might make a call one day when they have an emergency from my village to the city, and I think it will happen, because I have a very huge network that follows me.

Also, to give you another idea for the avant-garde, about six or seven years ago, a filmmaker in the U.S. had an idea to go to Wall Street and ask The Bank of America to give money back. That was Michael Moore. People were asleep. Five years later, they woke up and went to the same place, demanding the same thing. He was avant-garde. He was there five years before all of us. That's how artists are. They

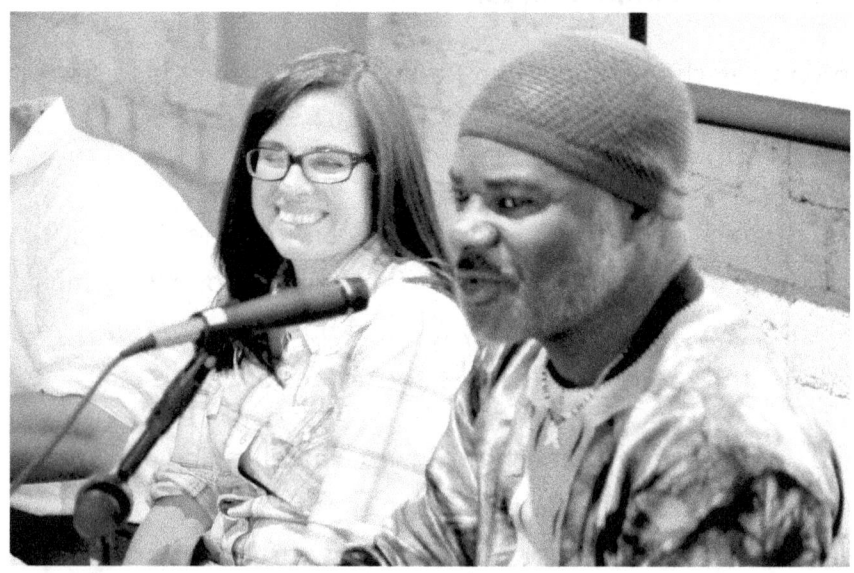

Paula Castillo & Issa Nyaphaga

show people the way. That's what I'm trying to do with Radio Taboo Project. If I wasn't an artist, I don't think it would happen at this level.

Michelle Laflamme-Childs:

Thank you. I'm going to move on to Paula, because I had a similar question. Although your website doesn't have that part filled in, I learned a little bit about your relational projects from Christy who talked about some of the work that you've done in the not-big-shiny-sculpture area.

I still had some questions about those sculptures though, and you can transition to talking about the other projects as well, because I know those are really important to you. The "Falling Petals Project," as an example, that's outside the biology department at Fort Lewis?

Paula Castillo:

That's right.

Michelle Laflamme-Childs:

A public art commission piece, it has a tremendous amount of back story to it. It's beautiful. And there's a whole huge pile of research and back story, and all kinds of stuff that goes into a piece like that.

My question is similar to the one I had for Issa: How important is that, in your mind, to the viewer's experience of the piece -- their awareness of all that's gone into your making that project -- or is it simply for them, an aesthetic experience?

Paula Castillo:

I don't know. [laughter]

That's the conundrum for me, with that type of art. I definitely start with a private, symbolic space. Hopefully, I'm permeable enough that my community comes through me in some way, but it just seems so inaccessible to some degree. Although it's a beautiful object...

Michelle Laflamme-Childs:

It is really beautiful.

Paula Castillo:

It really is a beautiful object and I'm very moved by objects. Most of all I'm interested in how objects, like humans, are very political -- not in the same way that you're talking about, but in the sense of that they are agents in the world, that can both alienate and bring other entities towards them, they can compose, they can generate, they can negotiate space.

Like Christy was talking about earlier today, I love making objects, and it's a real conflict for me, in terms of what I saw at a certain point in my practice that, as an artist, it was just like this narrow corridor of access.

It was very debilitating to me. I almost felt like I was becoming a cannibal with my own work, that I produced stuff, and then a year came and I was producing more stuff, and it's just stuff, stuff... and it began to become very alienating.

It is interesting too, with public work -- which is different from gallery work, and I also do gallery work as well -- It's for public space, but public space is really not public, what you were talking about too. It's often framed as these democratic spaces, and in reality, they are very passive spaces.

In combination with institutions -- that do wonderful work, like your organization, the mission is wonderful, but the reality of it may not parallel what the mission is in on some level. For example, an artist may have an idea that is a little too edgy. It's going to go through committees. It's going to be refined. It's going to be edited. It's going to become very passive.

In fact, that's one of the personal catalysts for -- I continue to do that kind of work because I love it -- but it was a catalyst for trying to broach that difficulty. In doing some of these anonymous projects, it was really satisfying to find that I didn't have to be the author anymore, that I could become a participant like everyone else was a participant.

And also, you could embed antagonism really beautifully... [laughter] and I value antagonism, because often when we talk about democracy or community, we imagine these micro-topias which are completely false, and they can in fact become very authoritarian as well, and we have this premise that we have to hold everything together. And so no one is speaking up, no one is shouting at you anymore. [laughs] Which is really sad.

One project I did, it was actually in Santa Fe, it was part of

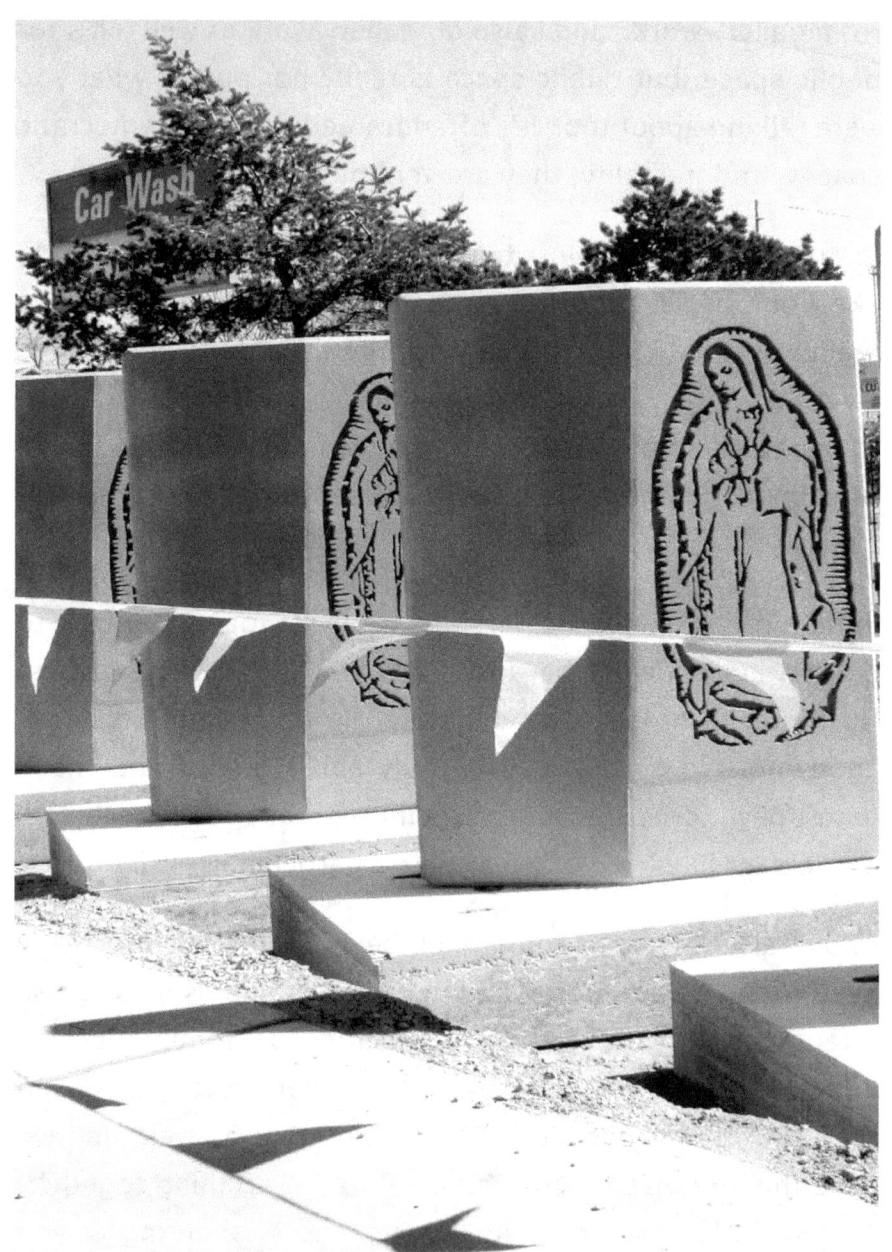

Paula Castillo *César Chávez Tribute*

a public school system here in town, the Career Academy. I don't know if any of you are familiar with it, right now it's called the Academy at Larragoite. It's basically a place for kids who've all been kicked out of Capital and Santa Fe High -- for whatever reasons, many of them for traumatic reasons.

This is why I say I'm a spy. I think all artists are spies. We go into places and we create these false identities, but they are all real. Fiction is real. I have taught in Santa Fe -- I don't normally tell a lot of people about this, but I can teach a lot of things -- I was teaching Algebra II, in this school. I realized that it was a great environment to do one of these anonymous projects. It was just like this very communal thing. It's interesting like this relationship that forms. Are you part of this hierarchy, or are you a participant? How do you do it? As an adult it's easy with kids, because it's established in our culture that adults do have some kind of authority. It is a natural authority. It doesn't feel oppressive on some level, particularly as a schoolteacher.

I would listen to their issues, and one of their issues was that they would get pissed off when they hold these food drives in Santa Fe, by what they perceived as affluent groups in town, particularly private schools in town, gifting things to them.

When they were little, they really loved it. They loved getting the turkey for Thanksgiving, and all the canned goods and the coats, and maybe that great little generic Christmas present or something. But as they got older, it was a burden for them, psychologically, because it didn't allow for their expression of compatible power.

Together, we created this project. It was called, The Gift Returned. It was a collaboration that we did with a private school in Santa Fe. We actually gave them a gift, that was object based. The kids, they wanted to do... You remember those little things that you did when you were a kid, like... [motions with fingers]

[laughs] Cootie Catchers! They created this really beautiful box, and then they made several of them and put them in the box, and printed this really lovely little structure in the box, and they sent it to a school. Basically, you opened it up, and there were things like, "Would you be my friend if you knew that I had an abortion?" "Would you be my friend if you knew my two brothers were heroin junkies?" It was a really interesting project. We actually never got anything back from this particular place. [laughter]

There were other projects that I did with these kids, but the

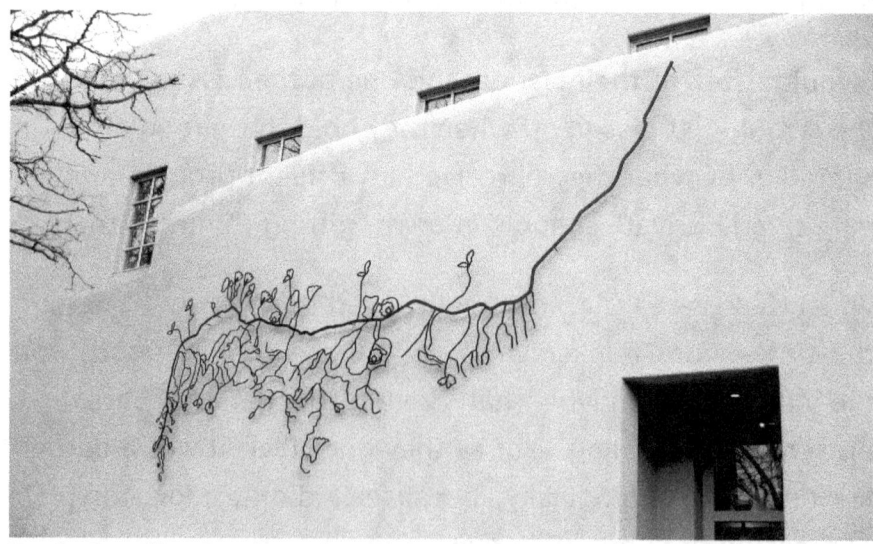

Paula Castillo, *Rio Grande Colcha* at New Mexico History Museum

182

thing that was poignant for me about it ... and I call this new-genre public work, whereas the shiny public work that I do, (it's really not that shiny), but the other public work that I do, I just cannot do this at all. No matter how hard I try with the research... In fact the project here in Santa Fe, The New Mexico History Project -- it really does touch on a lot of things that a lot of people were talking about today. But it just becomes a pretty shiny object, and there's no engagement.

My point is this, that, with these other types of projects, the thing that is so satisfying to me, is that in communities -- not the micro-topias -- but in real communities, there are dominant cultures.

And the things about these new-genre projects that is activated, is true voice; not just completing your own vision as an artist, but where partial identifications can be elaborated on, particularly by people who are not part of dominant culture. I don't know if I answered your question.

Michelle Laflamme-Childs:

Absolutely. The question is just a jumping off point for you to talk about these exact things. Thank you for that. I don't want to rush, but I know we don't have that much time, and I want to make sure I get to Sanjit and Jerry, whose questions were related. I can't decide who to go to next. Does anyone wish to go next? Okay, since you are sitting right next to me, I'm going to go to Sanjit.

[laughter]

Really, to me -- and I don't know you well, although I did have to research you at one point -- You Sanjit, to me, have beautifully integrated your personal and professional practices. That is to be acknowledged and commended. It's just incredible.

You haven't been at Santa Fe Art Institute long enough for me to have a solid question about what's going on there, but your work at California College of the Arts and the Art and Public Life Program is incredible. Not only can you find some of those projects on their website, but on your personal website, which speaks to that integration.

Two projects, in particular: Impact was one of them, the Impact Awards, the other one, where the young people went into the communities...

Sanjit Sethi:

Engagement.

Michelle Laflamme-Childs:

Thank you!

Those are really important projects, to me, in relation to the kinds of work we are talking about specifically. What I wanted to ask you, because you did that in the confines of -- and I know you left to escape those confines in some ways -- but you did that in the confines of a pretty structured environment of a university, of a school.

The struggle that I personally am experiencing, coming from

the organization like The Art Institute, where for me art was all about social engagement, environmental responsibility, cultural freedom and those kinds of things, and art as a catalyst for social action and social change, to a state-funded, public art institution, is to try to figure out how to do exactly what you've done.

So I'm wondering if you can talk a little bit about your experience, and any thoughts you might have about working in, and around, and between, and amongst those kinds of structures, to be able to do the amazing kinds of work that you do.

Sanjit Sethi: Sure. At one point in time, I was a professional student. I have an MFA, and I taught for a while. My parents were relieved, they thought that I had a full time, paying job -- of course, what did I do a year later, but I went back to grad school.

I went back to grad school to get a second master's degree, and this time it was at MIT. I taught a lot of undergraduates, I taught there for a couple years after, and their world is eclipsed by the idea of problem sets. They're getting problem sets all the time from most of their other classes. The classes that I taught were maybe the poetic release, and the kind of a free space with its own different set of problem sets.

The reason that I'm bringing that up is that I understand the world of problem sets, in the sense that I think it's important to understand, what are your parameters? It could be, that you're working within an institution of higher education like

I did at California College of the Arts. It's an elite, private, art and design institution, yet somehow had the foresight to

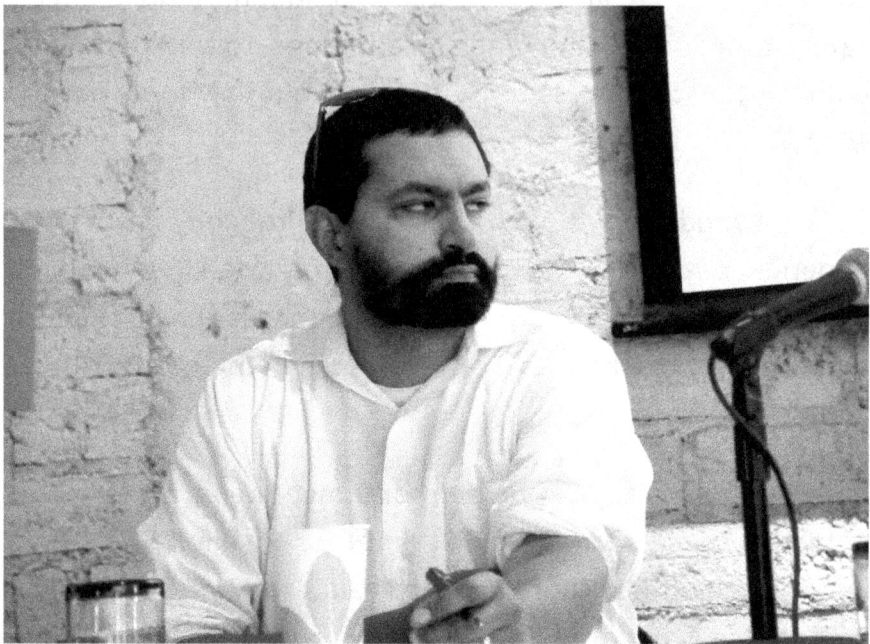

Sanjit Sethi

set up something called The Center for Art and Public Life, and fund that organization.

You could say, We're elite, there's no point in us engaging with the community, we should just pack up and go home. We have no place to take these elite, these kids from these different backgrounds -- actually, quite a few of them are socio-economically diverse -- but, it's not our place to go ahead and put them into communities.

I guess I disagree with that. For me, it's about the intentfulness with which you go ahead, and the method of your approach, in a sense that you recognize your limitations. You recognize, what can a 14-week semester and a group of industrial design students do with an organization that's focused on being a culinary incubator to low income, minority women, to create their own catering businesses.

If you start to understand your parameters, if you start to go ahead and really start from a meaningful exchange of dialogues, and believe that you're able to really take the time to exchange values, then oftentimes, you can really get a meaningful exchange.

You can get risk-taking and all of those things that are beneficial. I think you have to go ahead... I would work with my team and I would tell them, "Okay, over the next two hours, we're not going to say the word 'art'. We're not going to say the word 'community'. And if you do, put a dollar in the jar." [laughter]

And I think that's really true. You have to be incredibly cautious of the language. You have to look at -- we used to call them at the Center for Art and Public Life -- shelves, in a sense. You can't rest on shelves. You can't use "community""as a shelf. You have to really ask yourself what do you really need. Don't just go ahead and rely on that.

That may not square with grantors, you know when you're writing grants. Oftentimes, they want to hear the word "community", or they want to hear the word "art." But, internally, and I think that's true at SFAI right now, is that we're trying to scrub our language; "creative practitioner'" versus 'visual artist', because we don't know what a "visual artist" means anymore.

It really is about that care, and that exchange of values. I also think it's about process. We sponsored a project -- and I still vividly remember presenting this to a group of faculty members. We managed to get some capital investment to create a social entrepreneurship award program, and I remember the idea was to foster collaborative student teams to go ahead and create a partnership with a local, national, or international organization to do a project. And they would compete for three awards of $10,000 each.

I remember talking to some faculty members to try to pitch this to them, to get their students involved, and they were saying, "That's not the way I want to do it. I cut my teeth on waiting tables, and whatever else."

I really felt like it was a model to say that, "I want better for my students than I did when I was in grad school, or when I was in art school." I think that's the idea of, "How do you create new models?"

Outside the Stanford Design School, if you walk in, there's a sign that says, "Fail big." I would say that "Fail big, while you're operating with care," is probably my missive. But I think it's important to try things, and to fail at them, as long as you're open and honest about what your process is.

Because with as many successful projects that we had, we had some failures. I think the reason why the failures ended up helping add towards the successes of the programming, was the approach we took the failures in. I think that's really important. I'm not sure it's about oversimplification. I don't think it's about simplifying things, with working with communities, necessarily. I think sometimes it's about explaining things.

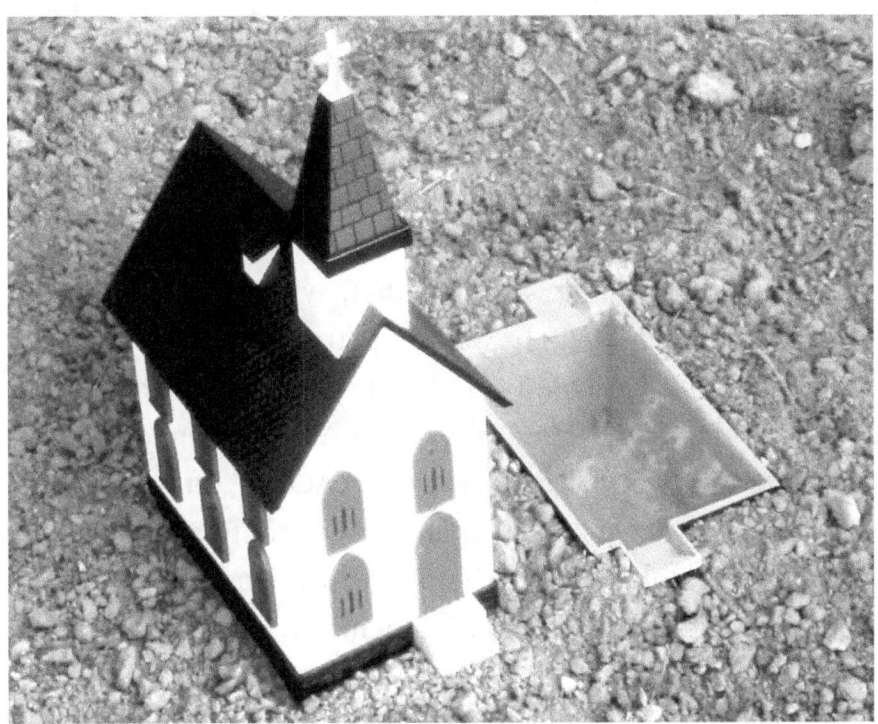

Sanjit Sethi *Architecture of Inversion*

I think that bringing an outsider perspective can be refreshing. It could be a vantage point. Anyone that's involved in territories around mediation can know the fact that being an outsider means that you're not Protestant, or Catholic. A friend of mine from Bangalore, India went and did a project in Belfast, and I thought it was great, because he was really visual. You could tell, he's okay. He's not on one side or the other, and I think that that's important.

I think it's the method in which you take that approach. It's the method, the care that you take in undertaking those partnerships. Are you truly listening? How are you presenting an idea that you think could be a catalyst for a greater sense of dialogue? For me, that's the basic premise of my approach.

Gosh, I think of soft projects that have occurred in hard spaces. One of my favorites, that I never saw myself, but it felt like I was probably really affected by, was the AIDS Quilt.

The AIDS Quilt, and its alignment with ACT UP at the time, was this very visionary project that, when it was installed on the National Mall, it was this tremendously cathartic moment. That we could go ahead and start to grieve, and understand the true immensity of the AIDS epidemic. It came alongside that activist culture around ACT UP. It was soft. It was personal. It was really an incredible contrast against the Washington Monument. That structure was made by this dominant, white male, king of hegemony.

It's projects like those, for me, that I think really stand out. The other one, for me, that is really as much a design project, and as much an art project, as it is I think a social activist project is -- I'm not sure how many of you know about Women on Waves, which was this design project about how you can go ahead and provide abortion and similar healthcare services to women that had been denied, by putting medical facilities on to a boat, and taking the boat twelve nautical miles into international waters. It's as much a design project in a sense.

Those were, for me, markers, to say, how are you skillfully operating within this territory? How are you identifying people that you think you can affect? How are you treading with care, but also leaning in towards a personal degree of urban acumen that one possesses to take risks?

Michelle Laflamme-Childs:

This ostensibly is a conversation about "public" art, or arty things that happen in public, however we want to look at it. Jerry, when I think of the work of yours that I know -- it's very intimate to me, the drawings in particular. You were talking about how you think it's small, but I think of it as very, very intimate. Yet, your involvement with Axle, in a way, has taken what is for many people intimate work, and made it very public.

Axle is so the epitome of "meet people where they are." You, instead of inviting people to come to a gallery that they will likely never walk into, you're going to park that step van, that accessible semi-beat-up, beautiful, amazing truck, and just park it somewhere, and people walk by, and some of the works, some of the projects, they don't require entry. You can experience some of them simply from the outside of the van.

I was really interested in that idea, that taking such a private -- what has been such an internal white box thing, and bringing it out into public. That was one thing I wanted to talk about.

Another thing, you mentioned in some of the questions, is the commodification of art.

Again, my own interest in much of this is that these projects are the kind of public art that I firmly and truly believe in, and yet I work in an institutionalized system where I have to have an object to be able to fund somebody.

Because the public art funding, the way it works in New Mexico, is they have to have a thing, there has to be thing at the end. We do all kinds of finagling to get around that, for instance to make a huge, temporary, amazing installation and end up with some little thing.

But I wanted to ask about that. Sensing or desiring a movement from a commodity model, to a service model, in the public art arena, and what your thoughts are on that possible transition. Is it entirely good or bad or neutral?

Then, the other issue that's related to that, is about documentation, because right now, often documentation of an ephemeral or a temporary project or a community project is the thing that exists after it's over. Is that problematic? Sometimes, that documentation doesn't at all represent what occurred in the engagement. There are two separate things there. Go, we got ten minutes. [laughter]

Jerry Wellman:

Well, let's talk about white walls and kindergarten. All of us have been to kindergarten, and if you recall the first three years of school, for almost all of us, what was our favorite thing to do? Generally speaking, it was art. And that's for all of us. So, the question comes along, what happened? Why isn't it out there? Why is it, that any given Sunday, there are several million people watching sports? Millions of people watching sports.

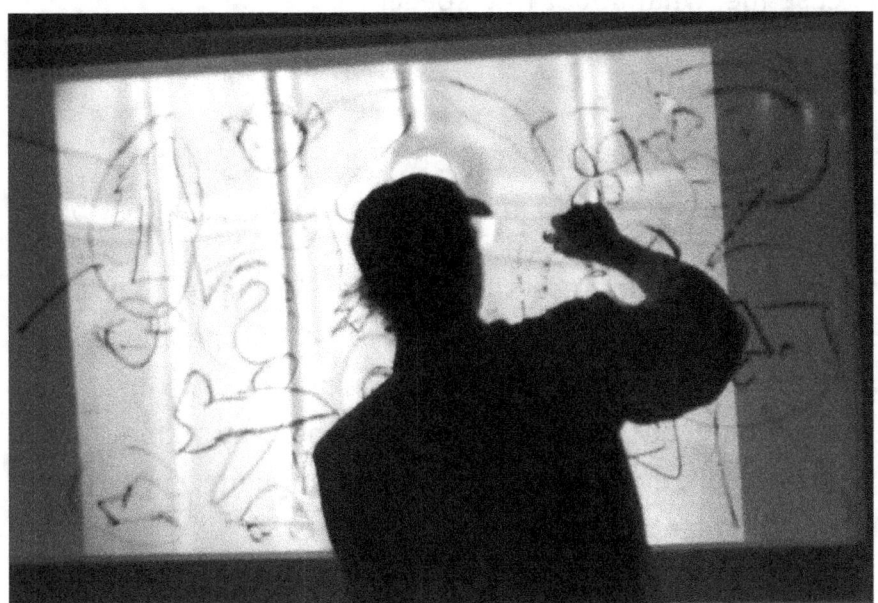

Jerry Wellman *Winky Dink's Unfinished Business*

There was an essay called "White Walls," I think. It was about why people are afraid to go into art galleries, afraid to go into museums. That certainly was a part of what motivated us to do Axle, and to bring it out to the South side and bring it out to anywhere we can. One of our problems is there are not that many pedestrian areas in this town. That's our problem. This model that we're talking about here could be done anywhere we would love to see it done anywhere, where there is more pedestrian traffic, and perhaps where shopping centers -- another difficulty -- oftentimes the shopping centers are owned by some guy in Texas or Indiana, or lord knows where. They're not going to give us permission to park in their shopping center for long. And I respect that, it's theirs, but nonetheless, we're offering something here.

Issa Nyaphaga:

Excuse me. What about free speech?

Jerry Wellman:

Free speech? Like what Christy did in Washington? Yeah maybe, I haven't looked into that too much, it's a possibility.

I also want to address the fact that I believe that art is really fundamental. I'm hearing a lot of people talking about creating politics or policies or different things. Once again, going back to kindergarten, and why I think art is fundamental, everybody loves that language. Everybody speaks that language.

Maybe through the presentations that Axle brings, or what we can do as artists, is to empower, and honor, and inspire. I really want to emphasize - inspire. It's through that basis of inspiration that political activity can come from.

I don't know. You got to have both. You do have to have someone screaming at you saying, "This is fucked!" But you also need to inspire people, too. Art works in both ways. Let's see what else. Commodity. Art as a commodity.

This goes back again -- I really have been dancing with this in my mind for a long time -- if those stadiums every Saturday and Sunday are filled with millions of people, and more sitting at home watching TV, now there's a model to investigate.

I don't know. I'm offering this up to everybody here. What's going on? How can we do that? These people are like all loyal

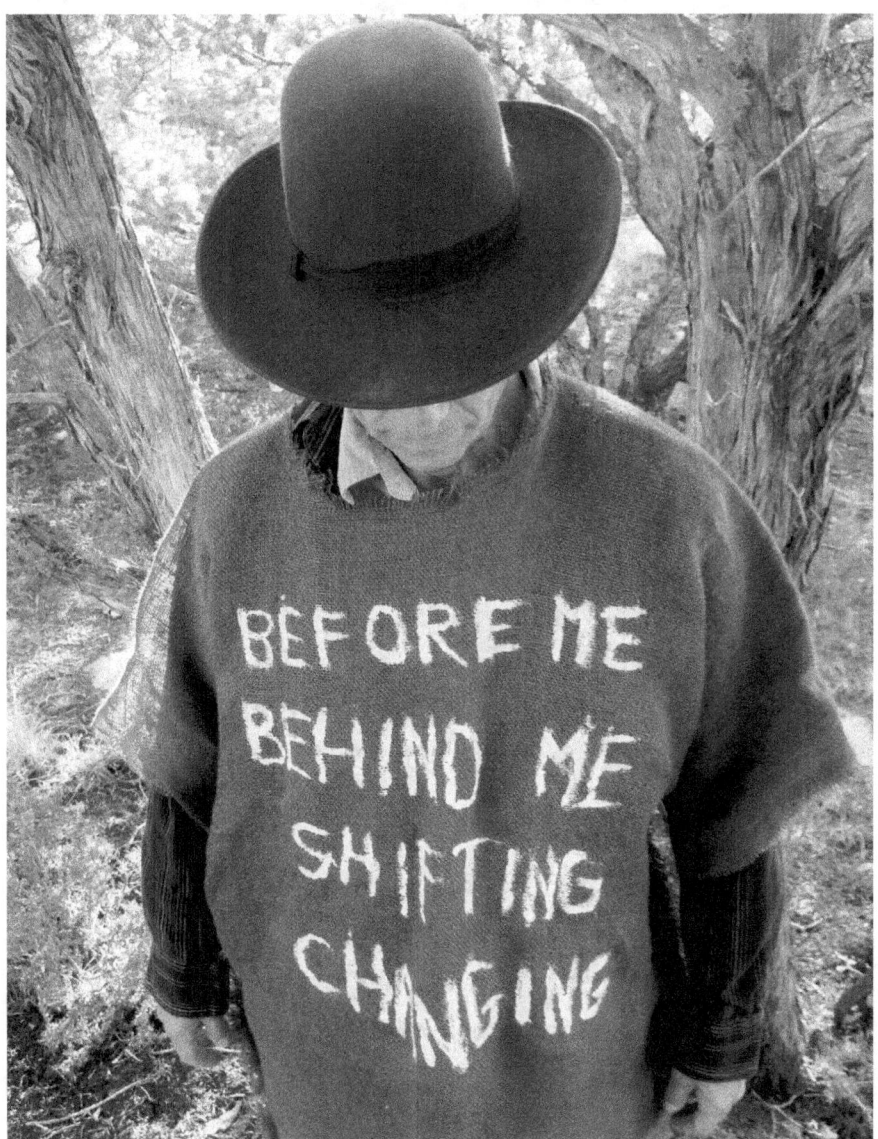

Jerry Wellman, from the collaboration: *Hidden Durations Operetta*

to their... I think Jerry Seinfeld made the joke, that he doesn't follow sports anymore because the teams move around so much, "I'm for the green and yellow uniform!" I don't know.

I want to offer that up. That's a model that maybe we could look at. I know that many sports teams do get funding from the cities, but they also make a hell of a lot of money in other ways. I don't know. Just, there. It's an idea for you all.

Documentation. Isn't this a terrific thing? Isn't this unbelievable? The worst thing about it is getting over my lack of the conditioning of using this. Documentation is pretty darn easy anymore.

What we've done at Axle, in terms of documentation, is we've offered new-school stuff, like social media, and old-school stuff, like books. Which also has very much to do with the wonder of digital media because you can do print-on-demand books, and relatively cheap. It's just a bit of a learning curve, InDesign and all that stuff. It's not bad, very time-consuming.

There's another issue that hasn't been brought up here, and that's that quotient that exists between time and money. Because we're talking about how do we fund this? Axle is largely funded by our time. That's an understatement. I doubt that we make federal minimum wage let alone Santa Fe's minimum wage.

There are other values here. I don't know how many of you were at the panel discussion that we put on last week. It was about public banking, municipally owned banking and time banks, all these different methods of economic exchange. Throughout the entire discussion, there was a theme that just kept coming up, and that's about values.

We're caught in a system that increasingly wants to quantify everything. We were talking about that earlier with El Otro Lado and working in the public schools, which is a horror of quantification. They call it rubrics, and oh, my God. That's another thing, that I don't quite know how to drift our policymakers away from quantification and towards qualities that make it worth it.

We all here know that there are other ways to address value, that's really what's going on. That's really what's worth it, not how much money we make.

Another question, about what is the public? When I was hearing El Otro Lado's presentation earlier today, I thought, "Well, you know what? Their public is E.J. Martinez School." They don't really necessarily need to present what they are doing to the larger public. If they can hit the school at a level where the people relate at to it -- here's a quantification -- at a level of 80 percent, that the kids walk away, and they feel like 80, 90 percent involved. That's better than a public art piece where people get maybe a three percent hit off of it. Maybe you get a thousand people to see it, and you get a three percent hit.

I'd much rather get 100 percent hit from 30 people. That has to do with how do we define "public". The public is a lot of things. This needs to be looked at in a different light than trying to hit something that everybody's going to respond to. It's very unlikely, anyway, to get everybody to respond to whatever it is you're doing. But it's worth the effort, I would say.

Vince Kadlubek:

The big thing I was going to say is, why is the art world so afraid of entertainment? That's the basic question. Why is the art world so afraid of entertainment? Of calling itself entertainment, of calling entertainment art? The public is engaged in art, let's not get confused. Video games are wildly successful, movies are wildly successful, television is wildly successful, fiction...

Jerry Wellman:

We're creative practitioners, let's just say that, it's so much better.

Sanjit Sethi:

I think Thompson, in an essay a couple years ago, wrote about contested public space. He kind of lays out the fact that -- don't kid yourself, don't go ahead and say that somehow being a cultural provocateur is the sole purview of the artist. In a sense we've ceded that with Red Bull interventions, and this idea of mass media outreach or product placement, and things like that.

This idea of provocateuring somehow being solely this nice, romanticized purview of that creative practitioner, it is gone. His position is, the advantage is, that that means that you also have the ability to run into territories that you would think... for instance, media production, etc. The thing that you may think is a provocative act may end up being a Verizon advertisement in the subway in Manhattan. [laughter]

So, I think that those barriers, for better and for worse, have long since eroded. Currently, it's an open field, right now.

Jerry Wellman:

Wasn't there some clothing manufacturer, I can't remember the name, some of you would know, who would pose ads with multi-racial people. They said it did more for...

Audience Member:

United Colors of Benetton.

Jerry Wellman:

Right, thank you! They did more to help the anti-racist sentiment - they were a player. They did a lot. That's another creative practitioner. Benetton, sure, what the hell, why not?

Paula Castillo:

For me, sports are really interesting. I don't do the large sports stuff. Growing up in New Mexico, we never watched sports. I have a kid who's very athletic, he's a big basketball high school player. And oh my gosh, I wish art could be half of what sports offer, because it's mythic. It's the hero's journey -- I can see why -- although of course embedded in that is the concern that it is the drugging of our society,

Anyway, that's definitely a concern, but I can see why it's so attractive. I guess it's entertainment because -- what is entertainment? How do we define entertainment?

Vince Kadlubek:

Something that is engaging enough to pay for, maybe. [laughter]

Something that's, yeah, I don't know how to define that. I know that we created -- in this building -- we created a giant ship and colored white trees in an alien world, and it was an art project. It was "Meow Wolf presents The Due Return," and we had people come in and say, "This isn't art." Yet we designed a giant ship, and we had 40 artists, or 100 artists participating in it.

We built adobe caves by hand, and we painted the whole thing, stained the whole thing. The thing was made by artists in many fashions, yet people left saying, "It's really nice, it's not art, it's entertainment." It's like, "All right, you guys keep pigeonholing yourself, man. You're going to have a lot of painting on walls that are not going to sell. It's going to keep getting worse."

Paula Castillo:

I guess the fear, I don't know, but could the fear of the use of the word "entertainment" be that it's quieting the masses.

Vince Kadlubek:

It's not smart enough.

Paula Castillo:

It doesn't bring up questions, perhaps.

Issa Nyaphaga:

For me, the bottom line is, are people who consume arts, sports, and movies, inspired? Are they moved, are they taking action? You have a commercial by Benetton, where people see it. They are moved. They change their views. Some of TV, it makes people dumb, it is not art. Whether or not they call it art, it's not art, in my point of view. We are people -- artists are people who are supposed to give meaning to things.

For example, when people say in Santa Fe, "I'm conservative," it's very negative. But when in Europe you say, "We have a conservative society," it's kind of positive because in Europe, they have a culture that everyone should have healthcare, everyone should have basic rights. Access of healthcare is not some sort of club for people. Actually, when you say this is a very conservative society it is very positive, they believe that everybody must have basic rights.

When somebody says in America, "I'm conservative," and "I'm defending conservative values," for me it's very offensive, because you're shrinking other people's rights. We are people who are supposed to give meaning to those things. My fear is that art might not be something that has meaning. You say you're an artist, and you're doing something that will move other people.

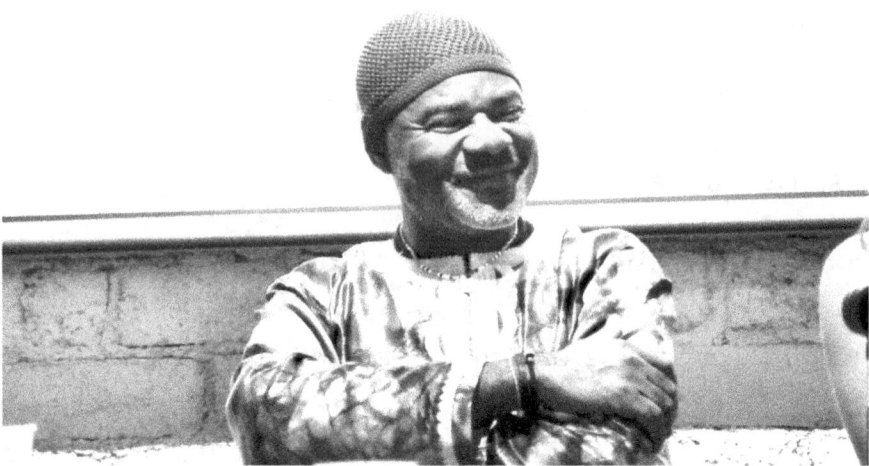

Issa Nyaphaga

You have a space in the highway where there's nothing, and some guy came and put some art, got the people to see, you can make art out of nature, out of anything. We're supposed to see that... and give meaning.

I don't want art to be like American taxes. We pay taxes, that are supposed to go to public services. Actually it's

funny. That space is our space, and we know in this country that the government doesn't have a Minister of Culture.

It means we're getting pushed out, we're being pushed into a ghetto. That's my fear, we'll become a very elitist club in the U.S. We don't really reach out to the society. We have to rethink, we have to rethink the whole thing from the foundation to the top, and tell people it shouldn't be this way. This is our golden age, we have internet in our pockets, we have it better than Picasso, because Picasso died thinking a phone needed to be connected to a cable. He didn't know we'd have phones in our pockets. That makes a difference.

[Break]

Michelle Laflamme-Childs:

I think we're going to get rolling. We have reached the portion of the program, where we open it up to you, people who have interests in all these areas or you wouldn't be sitting here today, to talk to these amazing people about what they're doing, or what you're doing, or however you want to frame it. This part is yours.

Audience Member:

Thank you, all, for your incredible presentations. There was something that struck me when Sanjit said something about that boat project. When Jerry asked, "What is it about sports that millions of people..." like, whoa. To me, the answer is in, everybody here is trying to get at, how do we get a kind of engagement, and the word community, which is a problem, but our sense of commonality?

When people are rooting for their team to win, they're having this visceral kinesthetic sense of commonality. To me, a community is ad hoc. It's an event, it's a process. As an activist, an artist, wherever words we use, we go in and try to create something. What we're to create, it's not going to last. It's an ephemeral thing, but it's a moment of trying to create. How do we get a bunch of people ten or 500, to say, "We're all on the same boat in this moment." Whether it's stopping to hear a bus go down the street, or whatever. That's what ties things together, for me, about what everybody seems to be saying. I just wanted to throw that out there.

Jerry Wellman:

I realized that as I was talking, one of the things that occurred to me, regarding the questions of ephemerality and commodity in art. We're talking about an old standard of a public art piece. Like a bronze of a General, or whatever. Art in general, especially nowadays, what really drives the art market is people purchasing it with the idea that it will increase in value. It's all about an object. All these things are objects that last. They are not ephemeral, they are not experiential.

But sports is completely ephemeral, or going out to dinner at a wonderful restaurant, that you drop 200 bucks at, with the wine and the dessert. I wonder if somehow we can begin to condition people's minds to purchase art with that same concept of ephemerality, that it's an experience. You enjoy the art that you have, pass it along to somebody. They may throw it away because they don't like it. It doesn't matter. It's all part of the experience.

Once people can start seeing art, not so much as a commodity that exists as an object, but more in terms of an experience. That's what a lot of the public artists that are here, and what they presented, that's the kind of public art that was exhibited today, for the most part.

Once the public starts experiencing things in that way, maybe we could start to generate more financial support.

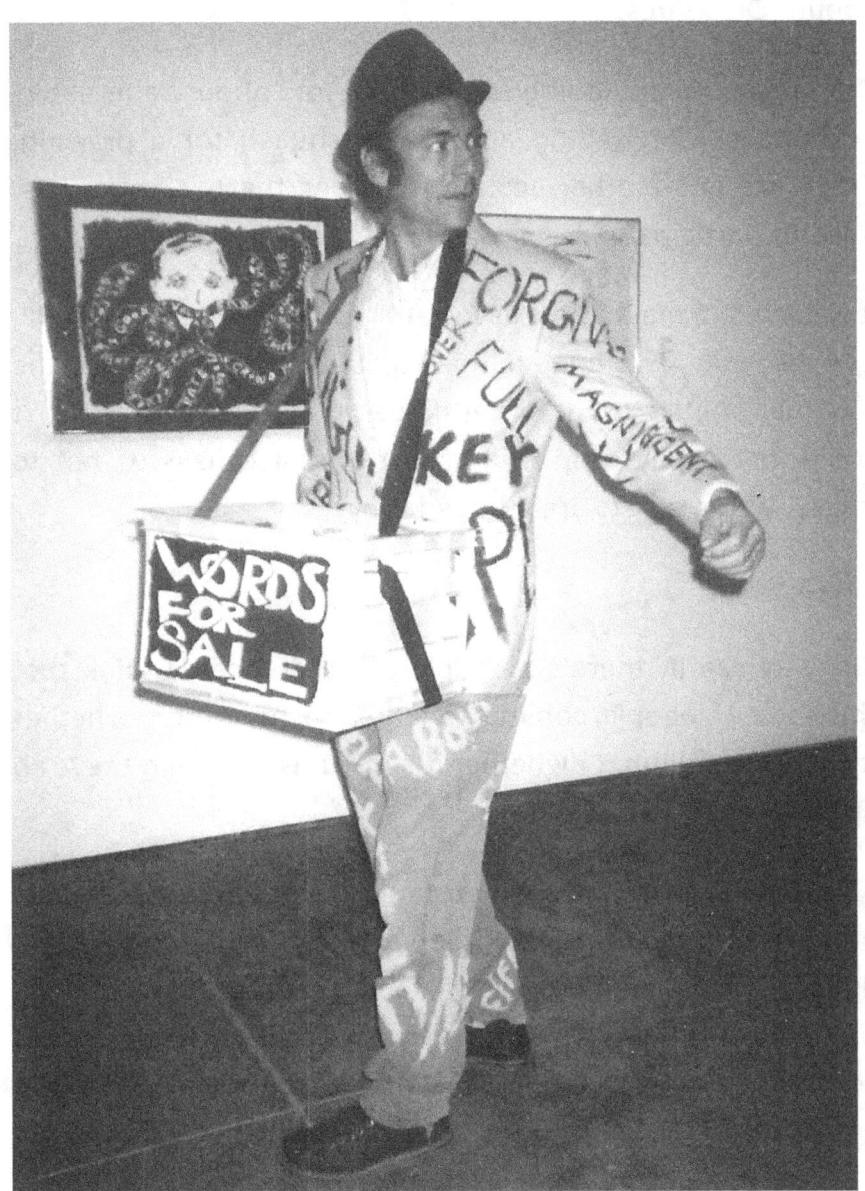

Jerry Wellman *Words For Sale*

I think that's the other issue that hasn't been really talked about. Or, values.

Our show Economologies had a lot about alternative economics, like trading a pattypan squash for a drawing. There are many other economic modes that we, as artists, need to participate in.

It occurred to me that the association of retired people, AARP, and the NRA. Two huge lobbies that absolutely massage the way that politics exist. What if everybody that was an artist could just finally drop whatever it is that causes us not to unite? We as artists are a huge lobby.

Sanjit Sethi:

The way see it, there's a couple of differences. I think that this idea of people coming together to be united, whether it's at the stadium, or whether it's in Tunisia, during the Arab Spring.

This idea of coming together could be because you're part of a larger broader affinity group, which then starts to, if not define, at least starts to soften socio-economic peculiarities, right in the sense that someone can be a Steelers fan, and you can make $240,000 a year, or you could make $50,000 a year, right? and you could be just as gung-ho.

There's softening, in the same way that you see in the Arab Spring, that you could have die-hard Islamists -- uncomfortably, but for a moment in time -- be working with people that are

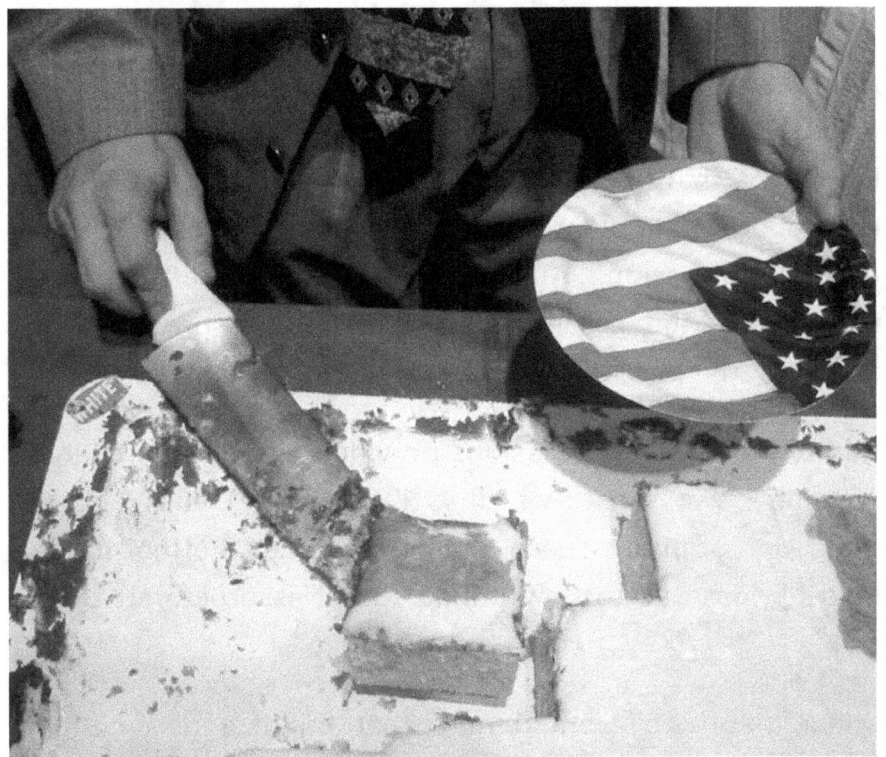

Sanjit Sethi *Serving Up Foreign Policy*

ardent about all sorts of different, diverse rights. Or Middle Eastern LGBT community saying that, "Well, this particular despot needs to go.

It becomes more problematic in the follow-through, and how they move forward together. But my point is that these moments in time exist. I think these moments in time have existed, with people being consummate actors within this, in terms of going ahead and promoting different things. I think some of the more prolific tweeters, and social media artists, if you will, especially in Egypt during Arab Spring, were pretty instrumental.

One thing about the culture here in the United States, versus a lot of other places in the world -- and I'm always careful to do this, because it's kind of easy to go ahead and pick out what's wrong with the United States -- but most other cultures, at least ones that I've spent significant time in, actually have, embedded within them, a way that they mediate public space through procession. Through some kind of regular activities that involve the procession of a saint, the procession of activities, the blessing of a fleet of some kind...

I think that those processions provide a conduit for a ritual, certainly, in a sense, which is kind of the reuse and the mitigation of public space, in kind of defiance of normalized kind of sense as to how public spaces is proctored by the state.

I think that there's something to that. I think a lot of cultures just have a sense of the physical activity of processing through public space to a particular destination. And I think there's something there.

Vince Kadlubek:

Just to dovetail on your thoughts on art and economy, and how the public fits into that, and reaching the public, and engaging the public.... the majority of the public doesn't have experience with looking at a white wall in my community to find familiarity with work that's on a wall. They just don't have a basis for... kids definitely don't, and many who grew up, don't have that experience. So, it's unrelatable.

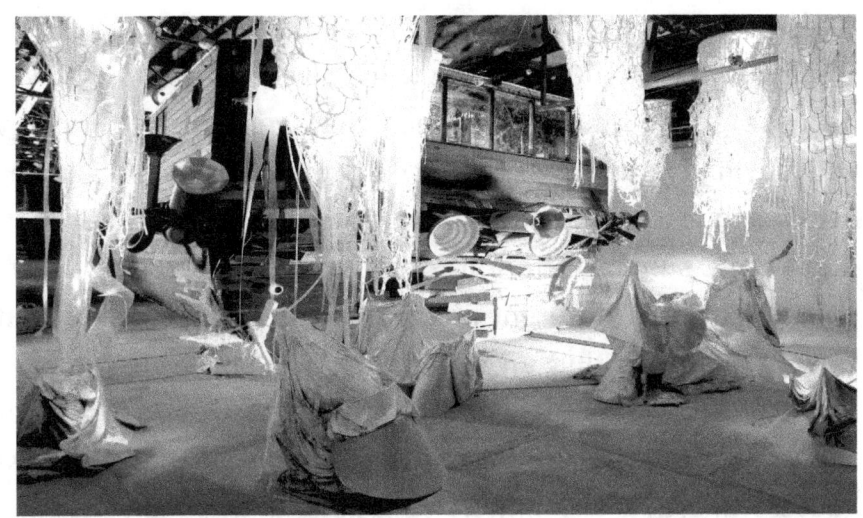

Meow Wolf *The Due Return*

And the format is based on selling. They're small enough, or certain sized things that can be put on the wall and sold. But if art stops selling, maybe the artist should start reconsidering their format, and their form. Meow Wolf was definitely a response to this, when we started in 2008, and creating maximal immersive spaces, which people do have experience relating to. A grocery store is a maximal, immersive space. Allsups is a maximal immersive space. Any space you walk into, you know how to relate to walking into an environment. We found that when we created these maximal immersive spaces, Any space you walk into, you know how to relate to walking into an environmet. We found tha when we created these maximal immersive spaces, people came that weren't normal art world people, and kids loved it.

People who didn't have an understanding of the art world or whatever, loved it. Then, to tie that to economics, the show that we did here brought 25,000 visitors in three months. We made $150,000, half of which went to CCA. It was because of the amount of reach that we had, and nobody was buying anything, except for the experience. And it was at $5 suggested donation, or $10 suggested donation. I know there's many different forms of art. I know that artists come with many different media to express themselves, but if we do want to find an economically sustainable model, I would look towards the world of immersive. If you looked at the art world right now, I think we would find that the most successful artists are immersive artists, that are alive today.

Audience Member:

I'm wondering, I was really moved by this idea of "fail big", and I wonder where that intersects with ethical bounds. I think we've talked a lot today in this particular type of art, and working with community, around... Molly gave examples of coming into a community and really opening something up, and then leaving, and the ethical considerations about that.

We've pointed to the trust that has to be built working in communities, and how hard it can be, and how much patience is involved in that. Part of what's inspiring about that notion, or that little sign, is that idea that this sort of work takes a courage, an ability to stick your neck out there and just try.

I wonder how you navigate that, maybe through your own experiences, or if you have any particular tenets or principles, with an ethical framework for also guarding against anything that would be more damaging. You spoke to that with that sense of acumen, how do you bring that into it, but I'm just wondering if you could elaborate more or give an example.

Sanjit Sethi:

I'll just say really briefly that, I think that it's easy to say "fail big." and it sounds cute. Your question is a really good one, which is to say, "How does it really meet up with the degree of trust, and the different constituents you're really working with?"

The first thing I'd say is that, in all the work that we do, whether it's my own community-based projects, or work that we do with our organizations, there really has to be an exchange of values, and that has to take as long as it needs to take. There really needs to be a sense, "This is where you're coming from, and this is where we're coming from," before you can start to approach that.

The most successful partnerships we've developed, have been ones where both partners are willing to take risks, and you have to be explicit about what are the risks you're taking.

It's actually meaningless for us, or it's a woefully inadequate partnership, if only one party -- It doesn't matter if it's the cultural organization, or it's the partner or constituent group -- If one of those entities isn't able to take risks, then there isn't that connection there. And you have to go ahead and reassess your relationship. It's from that point in time where a local organization says, "I'm going to commit 80 hours of staff time to this, and that's from a really meager operation, because I want this to occur." That's risk on their part, right, because those 80 hours could go towards doing a lot of other things.

If we go ahead and say, we're going to put our name on this -- and, we're a little concerned about this, or we think this is a little bit overreaching, there has to be an acknowledgement of what that risk is. That's when you're taking the plunge together, to a certain degree. Then you can go ahead and start, and then failure feels much more comfortable.

Failure kind of sucks, if you're not able to go ahead and feel like that, when you're talking about the territory of engagement, about failure, it hasn't got a mutual acknowledgment of the fact that this could fail, and what are the implications for that.

Issa Nyaphaga:

Well, I have to say some things: Art has a lot of power, in a country like this, it has a lot of influence. I live here because people understand what I do, and because they understand what I do, I also have my personal path. Let's say an artist does a social project or tries to engage a community, His. story is important. The way they engage with the process is very important.

I think, when we talk about failure, what I'm trying to say is that, in life, there's no failure. There is experience, there is exploration, but there is no failure. We just experiment with things, how do you gain experience if you never fail?

There are no mistakes in life. You just make a mistake, and then you know what not to do the next time. In a system like this, where we have a target audience, there is intellectual thinking -- between us and that audience, and there is the political system, that's also afraid of us. They want to make people into consumers. That's why we have people engaged in entertainment on Sundays. Because they want us to watch football. In America, most of the coaches in basketball or baseball are more well paid than teachers.

What are artists? Artists are teachers. People who try to open the minds of other people, by thinking out of the box. That is who we are, taking risks, because we are the first people in the West to tell the lawmakers and the politicians to recycle, that the world is going nuts.

That's us, and we are people who express something new every day: We deal with three things as humans: Gravity, time and space. Everybody's running to go make a living because they are being pushed. But we have to stop, people; and look at the world around us and admire the beauty around us, like the beauty of a piece of art. This is what we are trying to tell you. Doing our duty, trying to recycle, make a little farm, you know, eat good food. I don't know. That's us, and we need to get more people on our team. There's not only one art world, there are many art worlds, depending on what we do.

I've met some people who paint, but they're not artists. They're just painters. They know how to mix colors and do a great landscape, but nothing is moving in their work. There's no meaning, their work doesn't tell me anything.

I just wanted to throw that out there. [laughter] Because it's the world we live in, we don't want to be extracted from what we are because we are part of the whole energy. So we have to get more people smarter because we want to have a larger art community.

Vince Kadlubek:

Alysha, don't you think that we need to add more artists in politics?

Alysha Shaw:

I think we need to stop using politics [laughter] and start relating to each other as people, and that's the way social change happens.

But this is a question about failure and ethics.

Michelle Laflamme-Childs:

Did you want to address failure and ethics? You seem like you have notes.

Alysha Shaw:

I do, and most of them are from the previous question. For me, it brings up the question of evaluation. How do we evaluate the success of the work that we do, and who evaluates it? Is it the art world? Is it the artist? When you talk about ethics in this work, there's the ethics of representation. A lot of people, when they represent these kinds of projects, they're

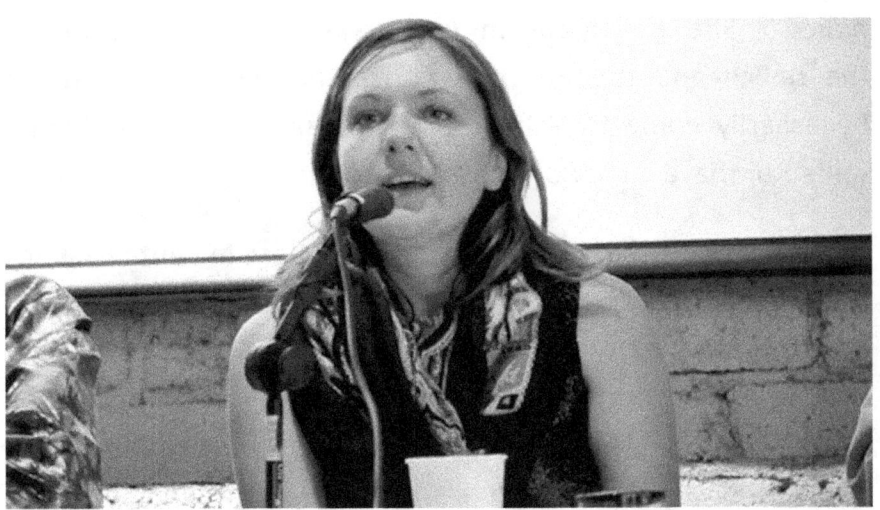
Alysha Shaw

like, "and the community came together." and it's misleading.

Actually no. There's a lot of complexity, that we'd all be benefited by, if it were more present in the representation of these kinds of works. I think that there's value in that. There's a lot of multidisciplinary action involved in these kinds of projects. The lessons that we learned from the failures and the complexities of engaging creatively in public... These lessons apply to so many more people than just artists.

One thing I did want to say before is the question about commonality. I'm more interested in the idea of plurality. How can we convene plurality instead of this "united we stand" bullshit?

Plurality: One piece that comes to mind is the work that Suzanne Lacy did in Oakland with the police and the youth. I want to know how she did that. She convened youth, who were targeted by the police, who were fucked up by the police.   She got them in conversation with each other, the police and the youth -- convening people who don't necessarily come together, and they sang and held hands --like Kumbaya. That's interesting to me.

The work that Creativity for Peace does, here in Santa Fe, with Palestinian girls and Israeli girls. That's really interesting to me. The complexity there in representing that, and evaluating that, and learning from that, and having it not be perfect or a cookie cutter -- that is more interesting to me than holding hands and smiling, saying it's all okay in the end, because it's not. This work is complicated. That complexity and that failure is part of the value of the work.

Michelle Laflamme-Childs:

I think Edie has a question.

Edie Tsong:

I have a comment.   It's around ethics, and failure, and assessment, and the public. I was thinking in terms of Snow Poems. For a public project, there's always this desire, you want to reach the most amount of people, the most diverse crowd as possible. Maybe that's a natural human thing to want to get the word out as far and wide as we can. There's also something regarding grant proposals, that you have to prove... You have to make this evidence for why your project is important. There's a certain amount of wanting to do that, so you can get funding.

When we were doing Snow Poems, people were throwing

out, "Oh, let's have poems all around the south side." And I said, "Well, who do you know there? What is the authentic relationship there?" Where is there authenticity -- that helps form your ethics. It was great that the librarians at the South Side Library were really excited about Snow Poems. So we had that there. We had a poem at Santa Fe Community College, because they wanted it.

But there was this gorgeous window on Fifth Street for Labor Ready, you know, big, huge, panes... as a visual artist, sometimes I make aesthetic decisions. I see a window and think: "Perfect, for Snow Poems." I go in there and start talking to them, and they're very excited about Snow Poems also. And we had a Snow Poem there, but the problem was Labor Ready is this national chain. That was one of the poems that ended up being taken down early, without their even telling us. That tells me a little bit.

This goes back to language, also. There's a certain way that we try to get money, because there's that system where the money is. But for me the question is, "Where is the truth in this project?"

So sometimes maybe the project isn't as large as it might be, maybe it doesn't reach out into certain communities, but it doesn't have to. It's just that each relationship has to be true, and real, and developed. If you don't have the time to develop that relationship, then that's   not going to work.

I want to say another thing about assessments, because I've been reading this Christopher Alexander book. He's a natural builder from Oregon.

It's along the lines of, "Does this make me feel more alive?" That's the question. That's not going to get you a grant, [laughs] but maybe you can find the right words for it.

Michelle Laflamme-Childs:

Questions out there? Thoughts? Thoughts up here?

Sanjit Sethi:

I have a thought, as we were talking about failure. Really quickly, I had covered it in a paper with someone that's tons smarter than me a couple years ago.

It was specifically on the territory around failure, within community based practice, and how we don't like to talk about it, because there are too many people to let down. You know, "Hey, X Foundation, I took your $20,000 and totally blew it," or, "Hey, I'm sorry," to the three different community constituents, "but we really didn't do anything, and we really didn't accomplish anything."

There isn't that degree of directness and frankness -- similar to the medical profession -- because you have to be so careful who you communicate that with, because you want to get that second grant. The system is inherently set up to not create a platform for that frankness, as to what's real failure.

I disagree with saying that there's no such thing as failure. I think the frank conversation has to be able to say, "No." Because it's not enough to say that, "We were supposed to have a community performance with these two different groups, and they were going to come together and perform, but we didn't because there was a lot of fracture, but we ended up having a potluck instead and it made us all feel good."

For this paper, when we wrote it, we interviewed two professions, where there was very much doing the profession, and then there was failing at doing the profession. They were professional pilots, and they were acrobats.

The idea was, there's a point in time where you need to do something else, and it's not being on a trapeze. It's to try to prevent yourself from receiving serious physical trauma; and in the same way, when your engine has stalled out and you're in a tailspin, you're no longer flying.

There's a certain protocol, and there's certain things you have to do, to regain the ability to continue on with the activity of being a trapeze artist, or the activity of going ahead and flying.

That's something to just toss out there, but it becomes... There are times when there is a rupture in normalcy, and then you have to think on a broader level as to how do you go ahead and regain whatever normalcy was.

Audience Member:

The idea of processional, that certain cultures have these set ways in which to occupy public space together, and alter it. I've always been struck because -- just in my neighborhood, down on the south side, there are these two moments in the year when I find it so wonderful.

Halloween, I could wrap myself in a sheet and walk around the streets. I don't, but people are out in public, and... you can have a commercial costume, but it's spontaneous, however you want to negotiate it.

The other is in my neighborhood, on the Fourth of July. And there's fireworks that are civic sponsored, but all these people take their lawn chairs and go out along the Yucca Street, where there's no driveways, and sit, and ooh and ahh, and chat to people they don't know. Which, like on other nights, you really couldn't do that. You just wouldn't.

So there are these little moments in our particular American culture, that it's okay to be out in the street, and talking to strangers, which is very interesting to me. We don't have a lot of public, pedestrian things.

But that's the kind of weird, intervention place, where I would look at: How could I, as a creative practitioner, find a way to do something with that already existing cultural thing? Everybody knows Halloween, They're not going to question what you are doing. I just wanted to share that.

Michelle Laflamme-Childs:

I'm a mere lowly moderator, but I would like to actually respond to that, and that notion a little bit, as it relates to traditional public arts. As a person who works for the state,

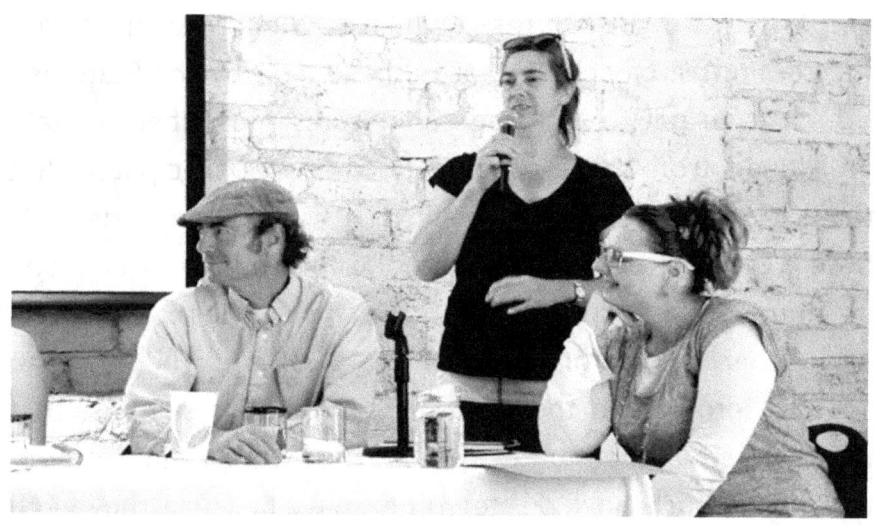

I travel. The way the state public art program works, in 1986, the state implemented a 1% for public art program. So every time the state outlays money for new construction, or renovation of a building, one percent of that money has to go for public art in that space. A lot of people don't know we have that program, and many of you probably don't know that there is six million dollars of that sitting out there, right now, that needs to be spent.

If there are smaller amounts of money, then that money is used to purchase artwork -- many of you have art in my selection pool, that I'm showing around the state right now -- but if there are larger amounts of money, there are commissioned projects.

Those, traditionally, have created things like bronze statues of heroes, or rusty metal Cor-ten steel sculptures, or big painted things, or landscape paintings behind plexiglass, and that kind of stuff.

The last two prospectuses -- which is when I go meet with the committee of people that is prescribed by the State, (so I don't even get to pick the committees prescribed, certain individuals from these organizations must participate). But the last two prospectuses I went to help write, coincidentally both were community colleges, one in Las Cruces and one in Albuquerque. Both of them specifically, independent of each other, asked for large scale -- $200,000 they have to spend -- projects in the central parts of their campus, that would create a community space. They wanted an art piece that would somehow create community, because they were feeling that, even on our college campus, that there wasn't an exterior gathering space where people were coming together. I find it fascinating that both of these organizations asked for such a thing.

They want public art -- they want a sculptural piece, they want a beautiful aesthetic sculptural cool thing, but they want to include ideas of community, and gathering, and learning, and all of these wonderful thoughts. And they want it to have benches, or a shade structure, or some way to have an art piece that addresses those issues.

That's where I see this stuff coming together, because maybe there isn't funding for some of the ephemeral projects -- that's really hard, especially given the constraints we have at the state -- but the fact that you can find ways to do these kinds of projects, within the structure of the system, is fascinating.

Really quickly, one other project that I was talking about at lunch -- if you don't know this project, please Google it. It's called "Open House." by Matthew Mazzotta, and it's an incredible art piece. He was invited by the Coleman Art Center, in York, Alabama, to come do an art project. His original project failed.

I won't tell you about the original project, but I'll tell you why it failed, to give you an idea of the community he's in. The town and York was so poor that the State took the lake away from them because they owed so much money. The project was originally a lake project, and that failed.

So Matthew goes around the city, he's interviewing all of these people in the city, talking to them. He actually set up a living room, outside, and had people bring couches and TVs and chairs and stuffed animals, and he talked to the community outside in this pretend living room, so they would feel comfortable.

What he ended up doing was, he noticed through these conversations, that there were all these abandoned houses, all over the city -- dilapidated, abandoned houses. He demolished one, with the help of community members. They completely demolished it, and saved all of the parts of it, so that the thing that he built was made from the reclaimed parts of that house.

Now, when you're there, you see a house structure; it looks like a house, a little bit like the one that was there, with the red paneling and all that. But with six people, it unfolds into a public performance space. It has seating, the city council has meetings there. They have public gatherings there. They show movies for free, and people come out. They have musical performances. It's incredible.

To me, that's another example of how you can do an engaged, interesting, important public art piece, that serves a community, but still have a thing, so that it can fit into all of these very structured public art programs.

Questions?

Audience Member:

Hi. Vince, I liked what you said about language. I know we like to think of language as something that brings us together, and allows us to communicate and connect, but it's also always been used as a way to separate and divide and mark the boundaries of community, and that's what we were talking about.

I think art is the same way. It has been, in the sense of fine art, a way to mark the boundaries of class. When we're asking, why people don't walk into galleries and white walls, there is a really good reason... They can read those cultural cues pretty easily.

And so, I wonder, when we talk about, "Oh, how do we take art out to these communities that need it so badly?" That sounds a little bit to me sometimes like, "Oh, we need to educate these communities, we need to better these communities. They need what we can offer them somehow." That's a really dangerous place to go, I think.

I think we're talking about something really entirely different than that, one of the metaphors that comes to me is art as medicine. We're looking at art as a way to heal certain things in our societies and our communities that we feel are broken. And in that case I ask, which are the parts that are most broken, and which are the parts that are most sick?

If we're talking about consumerism as part of that sickness, it might be to find, which is the most sick and ailing part, and what our audience could also be? I'll throw that on, I wonder if you have any thoughts.

Vince Kadlubek:

I have some thoughts based on some work I did with Mayor Gonzales' transition team. I worked with a five person team, working at the Community Services Department of The City of Santa Fe, and the Community Services Department split up different divisions.

The part that we looked at specifically, or that I was really focused on, was Children and Youth. The Children and Youth, through the City of Santa Fe, gives out $2.5 million a year to organizations; and we're not talking about family stuff specifically, this is specifically to children. A lot of our arts organizations in town get funding from their community services -- money, a bag of money.

They recently just last year changed things under the leadership of Carmichael Dominguez, who is the south side counselor. He was like, "What are we doing? Where are we putting our money?" Why are we giving Warehouse

21 $100,000 a year? What are they doing to better our community?

He started asking some serious questions. (That Warehouse 21 statement was my personal opinion, it wasn't Carmichael's). He was asking about a bunch of organizations,

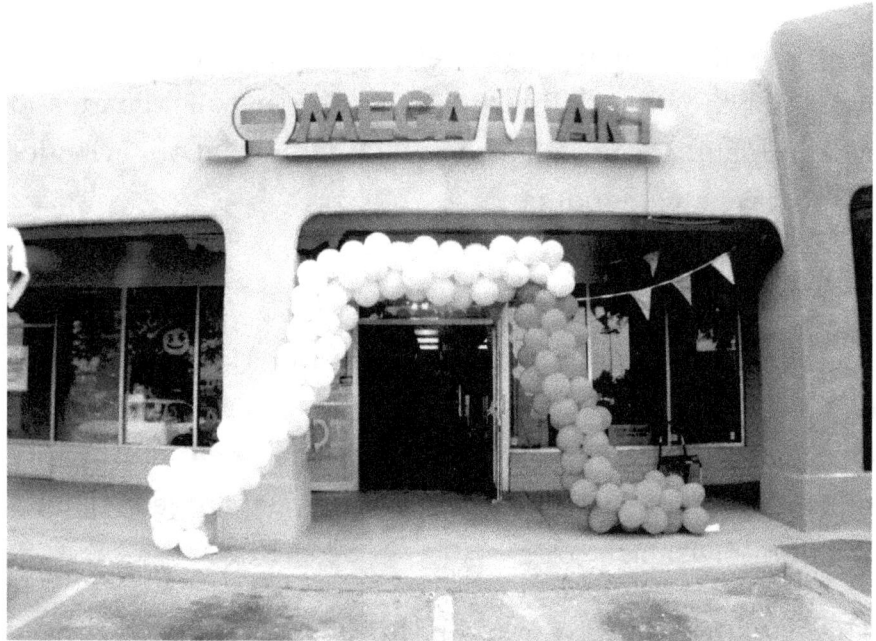

Meow Wolf *Omega Mart*

why are we just giving them money? Because they always receive it? Because they received it last year? What are the actual needs of the community, and how do we fund services for the actual needs of the community?

They needed to come up with some structure to decide what the actual needs of the community are. They went to a study by the Annie E. Casey Foundation, that basically determines, I think it's 16 key indicators of the health of a child.

Most of it -- it's in four different categories: education, economy, I think it's food, healthy lifestyle. Now the City of Santa Fe is basing their money that they spend in this part of community services, on Annie E. Casey's 16 key indicators, none of which have anything to do with art.

So as part of my piece in the transition team, and as part of what I was trying to communicate to Terry Rodriguez and Chris Sanchez and Carmichael and the Mayor is, I really do think that you're going in a right direction here. I totally agree that, if we're going to spend $2.5 million of the public's money on an annual basis to give to the community, it better go to places that is actually serving the needs of our community. But we have to write in some language that determines how the arts -- and maybe it's the role of the art community in this, of being able to help, to educate the city, where there is a shit ton of funding, to educate the city as to how art can contribute to these 16 key indicators -- how they can show improvement in these 16 key places.

And so, we know that there is definitely a movement away from art, and it's because there is a disconnect between the art-as-social-practice community, and then relaying that data to the people who are deciding the funding; How we can show data that reflects a healthy community because of art? You know what I mean?

Michelle Laflamme-Childs:

And it's 5:30. That's such a huge thing to end on, it kills me, but you'll all have to go to the dance, and have conversations over the loud music about all these things, because this is a conversation that cannot stop here, I think.

Really, it sounds corny and cheesy, and I don't mean it to, but I really am honored to be able to sit here with you guys and ask you questions. So thank you for giving me the privilege to do that.

Christy Hengst:

Thank you, Michelle. [applause] I also wanted to mention, which I haven't yet, that New Mexico Arts did give money, is giving money for this conference.

Michelle Laflamme-Childs:

We found a way!

Christy Hengst:

We found a way to have some physical artifact left... [laughter]

This is an art piece, this conference. The physical artifact is the transcription and the archive book that will be made, and published by Axle Contemporary, so that if anybody wants to look back... or if you want to share what was discussed here.

I look at this as a beginning part of this conversation together -- not that it's really the beginning -- but I would like to do this again next year, and see the conversation grow. Maybe we'll just keep on adding onto it, and also keep on making books. [laughter]

I don't know.. the archive is a nice way to have a record of what went on here. I feel like there is a lot, I heard a lot today. I'm really happy, and I'm going to be the person transcribing, [laughs] so I'm going to get to really absorb it more slowly too.

Thank you all very much.

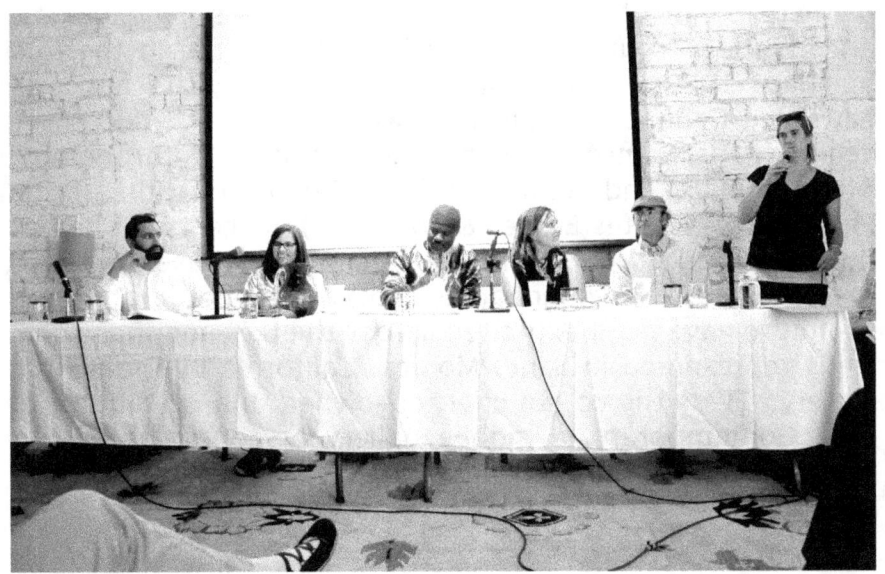

Paula Castillo

Born in 1961 in a small town along the Río Grande in New Mexico, Castillo's work recombines personal and familiar elements in unusual ways. The man-made microcosms combined with the expansive natural environment are the catalyst for her critical exploration of the systems and spaces we inhabit; places our own lives depend on.

Matthew Chase-Daniel

Matthew Chase-Daniel (né Chase) was born in Cambridge Massachusetts in 1965 and lived in New York City in the 1960s. He later raised tadpoles, minnows, and a raccoon, learned to fall off a horse, and hunt morels, wild violets, and rainbow trout in the Berkshire Mountains. In the mid and late 1980s, Chase-Daniel spent three years at Sarah Lawrence College in Bronxville, New York (B.A.), and three years in Paris, France, where he studied cultural anthropology, photography, and ethnographic film production (Ecole Pratique des Hautes Etudes & Sorbonne). Since 1989, he has lived in Santa Fe, New Mexico, renovating old houses, growing green chard, and making family and art. His photography and sculpture have been exhibited across the U.S. and in Europe. He is represented in Santa Monica, California by Craig Krull Gallery. He is the co-founder, co-owner, and co-curator of Axle Contemporary, a mobile gallery of contemporary art and vehicle for innovative methods of art creation and dissemination.

Michelle Laflamme-Childs

A native of the Berkshires of western Massachusetts, Michelle has called Santa Fe home for over 20 years. She is a poet and essayist, with one published chapbook and a book-length manuscript in the works. She is currently the Project Coordinator for the Art in Public Places Program at New Mexico Arts. When not working with AIPP to make important and exciting contemporary art accessible to everyone in our community, Michelle can be found spinning fresh beats on local radio station 98.1 Radio Free Santa Fe. She is an appointed member of the Santa Fe County Arts, Culture, and Cultural Tourism Committee and core member of the Santa Fe based Cut+Paste Society. Michelle holds a BA in English Literature from the University of Massachusetts, an MA from St. John's College in Santa Fe, and is intermittently working on a MFA in Creative Writing at the University of Texas, El Paso.

Christy Hengst

Christy Hengst's art work has been driven by love of sense of place, and by the potential of heightening perceptions in people. Clay has been the central medium in many of Hengst's site-specific projects, which include three art bus stops in Santa Fe, NM, a large sculpture project in Cuenca, Ecuador, and the 4-year international traveling public installation Birds In The Park. She is married an has two children in Santa Fe, NM.

Vince Kadlubek

Vince Kadlubek is the co-founder and CEO of Meow Wolf, a collaborative arts production company that produces immersive, multi-media art experiences. In 2015, Meow Wolf announced a partnership with Game of Thrones creator George RR Martin to transform an old bowling alley into an unprecedented, 20,000 sq. ft. permanent art experience in Santa Fe, NM.

Aly Kriekemeier

Aly is an educator, writer and creative collaborator in Santa Fe, New Mexico. She manages the El Otro Lado in the Schools program at the Academy for the Love of Learning and her work focuses on identity, gender, iconography and myth, border issues and post-colonialism. Born and raised in Big Sky country, she has a passion for the mountains and enjoys adventuring outdoors. Since moving to New Mexico through AmeriCorps, Aly has fallen in love with the area's intertwined cultural diversity, stunning landscapes and ancient history.

Issa Nyaphaga

Issa was born in Douala, Cameroon (central Africa) in 1967 and grew up in Nditam a small village of the Tikar tribe, in the heart of Cameroon's equatorial forest. As a child of the fields, Issa spent his time in close contact with earth and nature. Issa was introduced to traditional painting in his early childhood.

After high school, Issa started working as a political cartoonist, illustrator and reporter in a weekly satirical newspaper, Le Messager Popoli. His opposition to the political regime in Cameroon led him to several trips to jail in 1994.

In 1996 he escaped from his country to seek asylum in France. Since 1999, Issa has taught his painting and drawing techniques. Issa also has been working on the development of a philosophical concept called "Urban Way," in which he paints his body and stages live performances that include music.

Issa travels worldwide performing the Urban Way at artists residency programs, museum exhibitions, biennials, and universities. As an art educator, Issa engages in innovative art projects and conducts therapeutic workshops for at-risk and highly vulnerable communities, including children with disabilities, at-risk youth, immigrant families, teen suicide survivors, and child soldiers from Africa.

As a way of remaining in contact with his native country, Issa has founded Hope International for Tikar People (HITIP) www.hitip.org a non-profit, community-based organization dedicated to improving the quality of life for Tikar and Bedzan villagers and individuals with disabilities in the equatorial rainforest of Cameroon.

Issa has been the subject of several documentaries focusing on his life and journey. And has illustrated and co-authored several books published in the United States and France.

Sanjit Sethi

Born in Rochester, New York, Sanjit Sethi received a BFA in 1994 from the New York State College of Ceramics at Alfred University, an MFA in 1998 from the University of Georgia, and an MS in advanced visual studies in 2002 from the

Massachusetts Institute of Technology. His work deals with issues of nomadism, identity, the residue of labor, and memory. Sanjit recently completed the Kuni Wada Bakery Remembrance, an olfactory-based memorial in Memphis, TN, and Richmond Voting Stories, a community-based collaboration between local high school students and older members of the Richmond, CA. His current works include Urban Defibrillator, the Gypsy Bridge project, the Richmond Ceramics Workshop, the architecture of inversion series, and Indians/Indians – all of which involve varied social and geographic communities. After completing a Fulbright fellowship in Bangalore, India, working on the Building Nomads project, he continued his strong focus on interdisciplinary collaboration as director of the MFA program at the Memphis College of Art. Prior to becoming the Executive Director of the Santa Fe Art Institute, Sanjit was Director of the Center for Art and Public Life and Barclay Simpson Professor and Chair The of Community Arts at the California College of the Arts.

Alysha Shaw

Alysha Shaw is an interdisciplinary artist, musician, and community organizer based in Santa Fe, New Mexico. Shaw has studied and worked with performance and music for the majority of her life, as well as video, interactive arts, sculpture, installation, and writing. Shaw has worked on multiple political campaigns, social advocacy efforts, and community organizing projects. She is a student and performer of Balkan and Middle Eastern music, and has traveled to Bulgaria, Turkey and Greece in her study of Balkan music. Shaw has a B.A. in Political Science and Interdisciplinary Art from the College of Santa Fe, and an MFA in Art and Social Practice from Portland State University. Her current work explores the intersections of art, politics, and folk culture.

Molly Sturges

Molly is the Founding Artistic Director of Littleglobe, a diverse artist collaborative devoted to arts and social change. She is best known for hybrid projects integrating performance, creative exchange and social and environmental equity and health. She has created large-scale performance and engagement projects with communities around the globe for over 17 years. Awards and commissions include 2008 United States Artist Fellowship in Music, The European Union Festival of Culture, Santa Fe Opera, MAP Fund, Stockton International Arts Festival, Blackrock, New World Foundation, National Hispanic Cultural Center and many more. Molly is on the faculty of The University of New Mexico (Art & Ecology), The Academy for the Love of Learning (Co-Founder of Lifesongs) and is a national advisor on several cultural strategy initiatives (Rockwood, Opportunity Agenda).

Molly holds an MA in music composition from Wesleyan University. She has been an artist-in-residence with a wide range of communities including the Scotland's Art-In-Hospital program, Fathom (UK), and Gilda's Clubhouse (NYC). Molly is a devoted musical improviser and student of artistic experimental practices and community-sourced art making. She speaks several languages, and works as an artist-in residence, workshop leader, guest speaker and facilitator both abroad and in the United States. She is also a performing vocalist, recording artist, and leader of creative music ensembles. She has written and performed original music for a wide array of projects, including music for dance companies, silent films, circuses and sound installations.

Edie Tsong

Edie Tsong's projects in visual arts, installation, performance, and social practice explore identity as a practice of intimacy-- What connects us literally and metaphorically? How do we connect with each other as a community in our public spaces? Her projects have been shown at the Mattress Factory, TBA Festival (PICA) and internationally. She is the Founding Director of Cut+Paste Society, a women's community of artists and writers in Santa Fe, and is the Founding Director of Snow Poems Project. She lives and works in Santa Fe with her daughter.

Jerry Wellman

Jerry Wellman's first job, besides delivering newspapers, was working as a carny for Grover Bostwick in northern Wisconsin. His work as a carny, later a dealer in Indian artifacts, a minister, a tile designer and a videographer all blend into a visual and cross-disciplinary art practice. He has published several illustrated books, exhibited paintings, drawings, and installations, created performance pieces, produced video art and most recently co-founded an alternative arts venue, Axle Contemporary. His interest in poetics and expanded definitions of art is evident in all his work. Exploring and sharing that interest is central to his production as an artist. Jerry has an MFA from CalArts and lives with his wife and daughter in Santa Fe.

See slide shows, links to artists' websites, and the videos shown at the symposium at:

www.evolvingintentionsinpublicart.org

www.ingramcontent.com/pod-product-compliance
Lightning Source LLC
Chambersburg PA
CBHW080956170526
45158CB00010B/2818